READER'S DIGEST

FORCES
OF CHANGE

EVERYTHING IN THE
THE PLANETS, ALL
CONSTANTLY CHANGING.
NUCLEAR FUSION TO THE
ITSELF, POWERFUL
CHANGES, AND NOW OUR
A GROWING IMPACT. THE
IS THAT LIFE, THE
UNIVERSE WILL

UNIVERSE – THE STARS,

LIVING THINGS – IS

FROM GRAVITY AND

SUN'S ENERGY AND LIFE

FORCES DRIVE THESE

OWN SPECIES IS HAVING

ONLY FUTURE CERTAINTY

EARTH AND THE ENTIRE

CONTINUE TO CHANGE.

FORCES
OF CHANGE

1 CREATION

2 THE COMING OF LIFE

5 EVIDENCE OF CHANGE

6 DISASTER AND CHAOS

3 CYCLES OF CHANGE

4 THE SHIMMERING TAPESTRY

7 THE HUMAN ELEMENT

INTRODUCTION

NOTHING IN THE UNIVERSE STAYS STILL FOR LONG. Change on a mammoth scale marked the birth of the Universe in the moments following the Big Bang; change continues day by day within and on the stars and planets. A variety of underlying forces drive these constant movements and alterations in the stuff of the Universe. They include universal forces, such as gravity and the nuclear forces that bind atoms together; on our own planet, they include life.

Life drives the organisation of matter in ways that mark it out from the other **forces of change**. One of its special qualities is to combine matter so that it is **animated** from within. Life is hard to define, but it is easy to recognise – **living structures** are quite unlike the inorganic structures around them. As long as there is life within these structures, they continue to grow and repair themselves. And they have the power to alter their surroundings. As **plants** grow they remove minerals and change the make-up of the soil; they also affect the composition of the **atmosphere**, removing some gases while emitting others. **Animals** affect the atmosphere in a similar way and, being able to move, they have an impact on the land as well. Some burrow; others build. On the whole, however, animal activities rarely lead to drastic changes.

The one exception to that rule is our own species, *Homo sapiens*. Since **humans** first appeared on the planet, we have altered its face dramatically. By changing the land to suit our needs, we have pushed other creatures aside. Natural **habitats** have disappeared to make way for fields to grow our crops and rear livestock. Our ability to harness fire has had its own impact on the atmosphere. By burning fossil fuels and organic materials, such as wood, we have added **carbon dioxide** and other gases to the air and altered its composition to such a degree that global temperatures and climate patterns are now changing.

No other single species has been so significant a force of change on the planet, but the Earth has experienced greater upheavals than the ones caused by humans. **Ice ages** have come and gone, as have periods of intense volcanic activity and even bombardment from space. The planet has survived, and so has life. The creation of new species through **evolution** has been a continuous trend since life on Earth began. As long as the environment around it is subject to fluctuations, life itself seems bound to change. This ability to alter in order to suit new conditions has ensured that life has not only lasted on our planet but flourished, even after the most cataclysmic natural disasters.

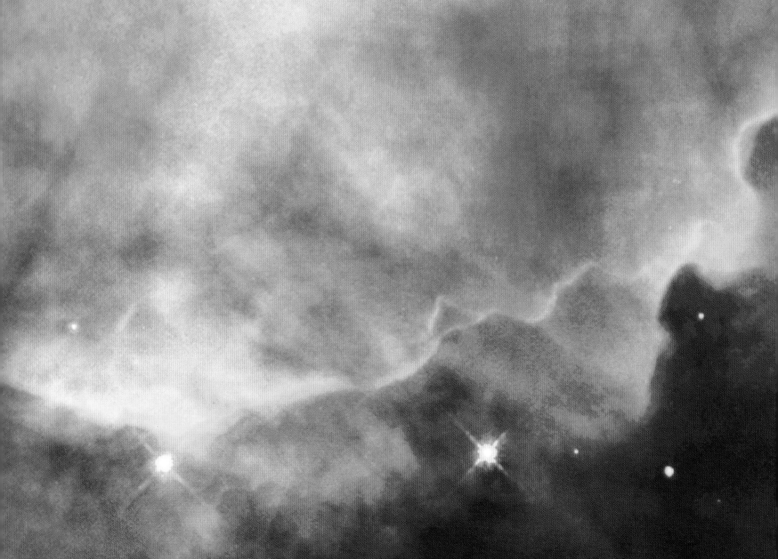

CREAT

ION 1

THE PROCESS OF CREATION IS NEVER ENDING. Although the universe was born billions of years ago in the massive explosion scientists call the Big Bang, new stars are still being created today. One hot bed of star formation is the Omega, or Swan, Nebula (left), captured here by the Hubble Space Telescope. The bright dots are young stars, formed from vast, incredibly dense clouds of hydrogen, oxygen and sulphur gases. The glowing, wave-like patterns of the gases are the result of the intense heat radiating from the newly created stars. The Omega Nebula is just one of billions of star factories dotted around the universe. Lying in the constellation Sagittarius, it is approximately 5500 light years from Earth within our own galaxy, the Milky Way. The Sun – our own star – and all the stars we see in the night sky are part of the Milky Way.

OUT OF DARKNESS

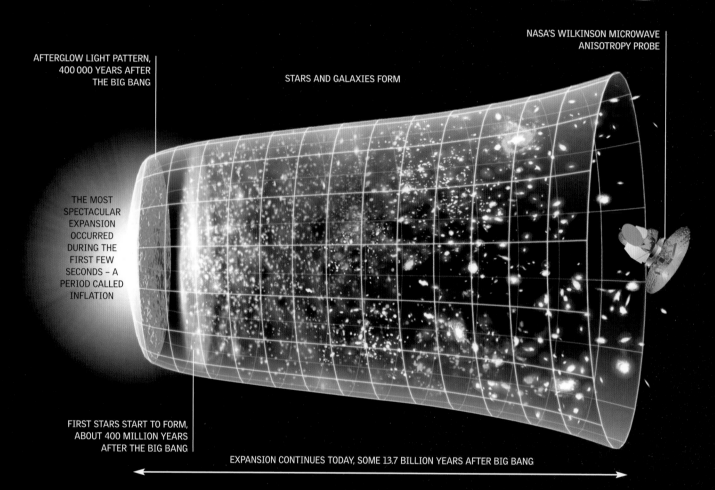

AFTERGLOW LIGHT PATTERN,
400 000 YEARS AFTER
THE BIG BANG

STARS AND GALAXIES FORM

NASA'S WILKINSON MICROWAVE
ANISOTROPY PROBE

THE MOST
SPECTACULAR
EXPANSION
OCCURRED
DURING THE
FIRST FEW
SECONDS – A
PERIOD CALLED
INFLATION

FIRST STARS START TO FORM,
ABOUT 400 MILLION YEARS
AFTER THE BIG BANG

EXPANSION CONTINUES TODAY, SOME 13.7 BILLION YEARS AFTER BIG BANG

BRIEF HISTORY OF TIME The universe's greatest expansion happened in the first few seconds after the Big Bang, when the earliest subatomic particles burst into existence. The first stars appeared around 400 million years later and the earliest galaxies around 300 million years after that. This illustration was calculated from data captured by NASA's Wilkinson Microwave Anisotropy Probe. Launched in 2001, it was designed to detect the afterglow of the Big Bang, known as the cosmic background radiation, which permeated the early universe before stars formed.

WE LIVE IN AN EXPANDING UNIVERSE. One day, scientists believe, that expansion will stop. At some point, far beyond human lifetimes – possibly beyond the lifetime of our planet – the universe will slowly begin to fall back in on itself. The moment it stops falling inward will be the end of time.

Time began 13.7 billion years ago with the Big Bang. From a tiny point of almost infinite density, the universe burst into existence, expanding at a rate almost beyond our ability to comprehend. The reasons for the Big Bang and the conditions at the instant it started are still the subject of speculation. What scientists think they can chart is the history of the universe from the first tiny fraction of a second after that instant.

In its first second, the universe expanded to 2 billion billion km across. At this point, it was filled with protons and neutrons, the two particles that make up the nuclei of atoms. These formed during the first ten-millionth of a second after the Big Bang began through the combination of much smaller subatomic particles, called quarks. As the rapidly expanding universe started to cool, a force known to physicists as the strong interaction or colour force pulled the quarks together. That force still exists today and is called the nuclear force – the force that binds protons and neutrons together in the nuclei of atoms.

The first atomic nuclei

Protons and neutrons existed independently for just over a minute after the Big Bang. Then, when the temperature had dropped to around 1 billion°C, they in their turn began to combine, forming atomic nuclei, through the process of nuclear fusion. This phase lasted just three minutes. Many neutrons had already decayed into protons and electrons before the process began, so there were more protons than neutrons. As a result, there were many protons left over at the end of the nuclear fusion phase.

The universe continued in this state, with free protons, electrons and simple atomic nuclei, for about 200 million years. Only when it had cooled to around 4000°C did the first complete atoms start to form. This happened as the so-called electric force (an attractive force between protons and electrons) pulled the electrons into orbit around the nuclei, creating complete, stable atoms. The electric force is weaker than the nuclear force that opposes it, which is why the electrons stayed in orbit around the atomic nuclei, rather than being pulled into them. To begin with, only light elements – hydrogen, helium and lithium – existed.

VISION OF THE PAST To look through space is also to look back in time (see box, page 21). This picture of deep space, taken by the Hubble Space Telescope, shows some of the very earliest galaxies as they appeared soon after the Big Bang.

THE COSMIC FLUX

GALACTIC CRASH This Hubble Space Telescope image shows the Antennae Galaxies, which lie in the constellation of Corvus. The Antennae are in the midst of a galactic collision. Originally two separate galaxies, they are now merging to form one supergalaxy. Astronomers believe that such a collision may occur in the distant future between our own galaxy, the Milky Way, and its nearest neighbour, Andromeda.

THE UNIVERSE IS ALWAYS CHANGING. Although the patterns we see in the night sky seem fixed, new stars are appearing all the time and old ones fading out. In our own galaxy, the Milky Way, a star explodes about once every 300 years, and the Milky Way is just one of billions of galaxies. Around the universe, a star blows up every few seconds. These exploding stars are called supernovae – they are short-lived, immensely bright and emit huge amounts of energy.

Stars are not alone in being subject to violent change. Galaxies can also be torn apart, stretched or battered beyond recognition. Some, like the Milky Way, lie alone in space and are currently safe from harm. Others exist in clusters, where collisions are common. The time frame over which these occur is vast in human terms, but the effects can be seen and even photographed (see box, page 21).

Gravity is the force behind such galactic collisions as well as in the creation of galaxy clusters. Gravity has existed as

VIEW FROM THE EDGE This infrared image from NASA's Spitzer Space Telescope shows the centre of our galaxy, the Milky Way, which we can often see as a faint band of stars stretching across the night sky.

a distinct force since the first millionth of a trillionth of a trillionth of a second after the start of the Big Bang, but in the earliest stages of the evolution of the universe, it had only a small part to play. Then, as soon as atoms began to form, its role grew. It was gravity that pulled the first atoms together into clumps; it then pulled those clumps together to form clouds of basic matter, from which the first stars were born. Gravity governs the movements of the galaxies, stars and planets, and affects every single living and non-living thing on Earth.

The first stars

The very earliest stars were short-lived and are no longer visible today. The way in which they formed was similar to the way in which stars form now, billions of years later, but the universe then was much simpler than the one we live in now.

At that stage, around 400 million years after the Big Bang, it was still very hot, and there was no light, apart from a faint glow given off by the super-heated particles in the gaseous clouds. Matter existed, but it did so in far fewer forms than it does now. Hydrogen, helium and lithium – the three lightest elements – were probably the only chemical elements, although it is possible that small amounts of the fourth lightest element, beryllium, had also appeared.

NEW WORLDS

THE FIRST STARS FORMED AS GRAVITY PULLED THE PARTICLES IN PRIMORDIAL STAR-FORMING CLOUDS EVER MORE TIGHTLY TOGETHER. By cosmic standards that process was quick. The primordial clouds took around 100 million years to form; it then took just 100 000 years for the first stars to condense from them.

Within these stars, heavier chemical elements appeared, such as iron, oxygen and carbon, and as the stars exploded at the ends of their short lives, the new forms of matter were scattered through the universe. Once the first stars had come into existence, it is thought that they set off chain reactions by which other similarly short-lived stars were born.

The first galaxies

At this point, our understanding of the history of the universe is hazy. The mechanism for early star formation is widely accepted, but the next step, the process by which galaxies formed, is far from clear. What is known is when the first galaxies began to appear. Observations made using the Hubble Space Telescope (see box, opposite) and the Subaru Telescope in Hawaii have shown that there were hundreds of galaxies in the universe 12.8 billion years ago. Looking 200 million years farther back, however, just a single early galaxy has been found.

Today, there are an estimated 125 billion galaxies in the universe. Although many continue to change, they stopped forming long ago – the Milky Way is thought to be at least 12.6 billion years old. Star formation, on the other hand, continues. Like early stars, new stars form from collapsing clouds of gas and dust; unlike the clouds in the early universe, however, these ones also contain heavier and more complex elements, the leftovers from earlier

STELLAR CRADLE The star cluster Pismis 24 sits above a spectacular nebula (cloud of gas), known only as NGC 6357 – after its place in the New General Catalogue (NGC) of objects in space. The faint white dots within the nebula are stars forming. It was in a nebula such as this that our own Sun and Solar System first came into being.

FORMATION OF THE PLANETS
The same process that gave birth to our Sun also gave birth to the planets of the Solar System. Around 4.6 billion years ago, the Sun began to burn in the centre of a vast swirling cloud of gas and dust (1). As the cloud spun, the particles within it collided, forming clumps of matter, which slowly grew (2). Gravity eventually pulled these clumps of matter together, forming the planets (3). To begin with, the inner planets in particular were incredibly hot, but over time they have cooled.

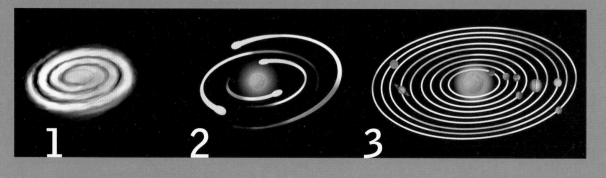

1 2 3

THE SPACE-TIME CONTINUUM

Time and space are inextricably linked – the one cannot exist without the other. Any movement through space entails a movement through time and vice versa. Physicists call this situation the space-time continuum, and it makes questions such as 'What existed before the Big Bang?' meaningless. Nothing existed before the Big Bang, because there was no 'before the Big Bang'. Time itself began at that point when space first came into existence.

Everything that we perceive has already happened. By looking at an object, even another person, through space, we are also looking through time. Most of the things that we see in our everyday lives are so close that it takes only infinitesimally small amounts of time for the light from them to reach us. Nevertheless, by the time that light reaches our eyes what it shows us is already in the past. This is what Albert Einstein meant when he talked about relativity. Time and space are relative to one another. The farther away an object is in space, the farther away it is in time. When we look into the night sky we are looking at stars as they existed millions of years ago. Telescopes enable us to look even farther back in time. With the Hubble Space Telescope we can see galaxies and other cosmic phenomena as they appeared not long after the Big Bang.

supernovae (exploding stars). As a new star forms, the remaining gases and dust in the cloud often form rotating disks, orbiting around it. These are the seeds from which planets are born.

The beginning of our Sun

The history of our own corner of the Milky Way, the Solar System, started around 4.6 billion years ago, when the Sun came into existence. Scientists think it was born from the collapse of a nebula, a great cloud of gas several light years across, which probably also gave rise to several other stars.

The nebula is believed to have been contained within an open star cluster, a group of stars loosely bound together by their interacting gravitational forces. The evidence for this comes from meteorites in the Solar System that were formed around the same time as the Sun itself. These contain heavy elements, which could only have been created inside other stars. The elements must have entered the nebula as the result of supernova explosions, which implies that there were other stars relatively close by. The open star cluster existed in one of the spiral arms of the Milky Way.

The collapse of the gas cloud may have been triggered by the shock waves from a supernova explosion. Whatever the cause, part of the cloud began to spin. The material in the axis of that spin was forced ever closer together, and gradually more and more gas was drawn in from around it. As this happened, the density at the centre of the spinning cloud increased. Collisions between atoms there became more and more frequent, and the temperature rose. The relatively small amount of material that remained outside the hot, dense central point flattened out into a rotating disk. After around 100 million years, the temperature and pressure at the centre of the cloud had increased enough for nuclear fusion to begin. This marked the birth of a new star – our Sun started to shine.

While this was happening, collisions in the surrounding disk caused clumps of matter to form. As these in their turn collided with one another, they gradually grew, forming larger bodies known as planetesimals. In the inner Solar System, warmed by the newly burning Sun, these planetesimals consisted mainly of chemical elements and compounds with high boiling points, such as metals and silicates. They went on to form the inner, rocky planets. Farther out, where it was colder, more volatile molecules, such as methane and water, were able to condense. They, together with most of the hydrogen and helium not drawn into the early Sun, formed the outer gaseous planets, each with its own rocky core.

Since the Solar System formed, most of the planets have changed. Mars, for instance, once had a rich atmosphere, but this has now largely been lost, blown away into space by the power of the solar wind. Earth, on the other hand, has retained its atmosphere, although the atmosphere it has today is very different from the one that it began with.

From life-giving Sun to white dwarf

The Sun is the great power that sustains most life on the surface of our planet, but eventually it will turn against the Earth – it will die and take our planet with it. This fate is not imminent, however. The Sun still has enough fuel to keep burning as it does

THE SUN AS A RED GIANT

The Sun is like a vast nuclear fusion power station, combining hydrogen in its core to create helium and generating an incredible amount of heat and other radiation as a side effect. Eventually, the hydrogen in the Sun's core will begin to run out, and when that happens, the Sun will start burning up hydrogen in its outer layers. As a consequence, it will expand. By the time it stops expanding, it will have changed from the medium-sized star it is at the moment into the kind of star astronomers call a red giant – a fiery furnace so vast that it will have completely engulfed Mercury, Venus and, quite possibly, the Earth. Even if the Earth escapes being enveloped, it will be vaporised.

SUN AS IT IS NOW

SUN AS A RED GIANT

BLOWN AWAY Today, only a thin, wispy layer remains of the once rich atmosphere of the planet Mars.

now for about 5 billion years. That is longer than the entire history of the Earth so far.

The Sun's death throes will be gradual. Seen from Earth, its disk will slowly grow ever larger in the sky as it becomes a red giant (see box, above). Inevitably, the Earth will heat up and the oceans will evaporate. The Earth's water will accumulate as vapour in the stratosphere, leaving the surface below baked dry. No rain will fall, and the remaining water molecules high in the planet's atmosphere will disappear – split by the power of the Sun, their hydrogen atoms will be lost into space. By then, life on Earth will have been extinguished. Even the hardiest living organisms cannot survive without water.

Eventually, the Sun will stop expanding and start to lose vast amounts of matter into space. At the end, all that will be left will be the brightly glowing embers of its core. It will have become what is known as a white dwarf, a tiny super-dense star no bigger than the Earth it once illuminated.

SOLAR FLARES

THE MOST POWERFUL EXPLOSIONS IN

THE SOLAR SYSTEM ERUPT FROM THE SUN WITH POWER EQUIVALENT TO SEVERAL BILLION NUCLEAR WARHEADS GOING OFF AT ONCE. They are called solar flares, and although they occur more than 145 million km away, we feel their effects on Earth: they can interfere with mobile phones, for example.

Solar flares are formed from super-heated plasma, the fourth and most energetic state of matter (the other three states are solid, liquid and gas). They happen most frequently around sunspots, caused by intense magnetic fields bursting up through the Sun's surface. As the flares roll upwards from the Sun's surface they accelerate the protons, electrons and heavy ions that they pass through until they reach speeds close to that of light. These particles then hurtle out into space as part of the solar wind. On Earth, the solar wind causes the aurora borealis and aurora australis, the northern and southern lights.

Flares are not confined to the Sun. Similar explosions, called stellar flares, have been observed in the atmospheres of other stars and are thought to be common throughout the universe. One such flare observed in December 2005 was so large that, had it come from the Sun, it would have caused a mass extinction on Earth. It came from a highly unstable star slightly smaller than the Sun in the constellation of Pegasus, about 135 light years from Earth. It released around 100 million times the energy of a typical solar flare.

VITAL STATISTICS

**AVERAGE AMOUNT OF ENERGY
  RELEASED:** 500 million megatons
**APPROXIMATE MAXIMUM
  TEMPERATURE:** 100 million°C
NORMAL DURATION: 20 minutes
  to 13 hours

OUR SOLAR SYSTEM

SCIENTISTS HAVE RECENTLY REDUCED THE NUMBER OF PLANETS IN THE SOLAR SYSTEM TO EIGHT. Pluto, previously regarded as the smallest planet, has been reclassified as a dwarf planet, along with Ceres in the Asteroid Belt and Eris in the Kuiper Belt. The Asteroid and Kuiper Belts are other components in the Solar System. The Asteroid Belt, between Mars and Jupiter, consists of more than 90 000 chunks of rocky matter left over from the formation of the Solar System. The Kuiper Belt, which extends beyond Neptune for about 1.8 billion km, is the source of comets with regular orbits, such as Halley's Comet. Surrounding the Solar System is the Oort Cloud, spreading out beyond the Kuiper Belt for about 30 trillion km. Held in place by the gravitational pull of the Sun, it contains countless bodies made of dust and ice.

JUPITER

MARS

EARTH

VENUS Similar in size to the Earth, Venus is also similar in its internal structure. But the conditions on its surface could hardly be more different. It lacks oceans and is permanently blanketed by thick clouds. Its atmosphere is made up almost entirely of carbon dioxide and nitrogen. This traps heat near the surface, lifting temperatures to an average 480°C, the highest on any planet. Like Mercury, Venus has no moons. Venus orbits the Sun once every 224.7 days and rotates on its axis once every 243 days.

EARTH The presence of life means that Earth is by far the most varied planet in the Solar System, at least on its surface. It is the only planet known to have oceans of liquid water and the only one known for certain still to be geologically active. Its Moon is the 14th largest body in the Solar System. Earth orbits the Sun once every 365.3 days and rotates on its axis once every 23 hours and 56 minutes.

MERCURY The smallest of the eight planets is slightly smaller in diameter than Ganymede or Titan, the largest moons of Jupiter and Saturn, respectively, but it has more than twice the mass of either. It has a large iron core and generates its own magnetic field, about a tenth the strength of that generated by Earth. Its surface is solid and heavily cratered. Mercury orbits the Sun once every 88 days and rotates on its axis once every 58.7 days.

MERCURY

VENUS

MERCURY   EARTH

MARS Early in its history Mars is thought to have had similar surface conditions to Earth's. Today, however, it is barren and its atmosphere is thin. What gas exists near its surface (mainly carbon dioxide) is often whipped up into ferocious winds. Its diameter is just over half Earth's. It rotates once every 24 hours and 37 minutes, and takes 687 days to orbit the Sun. Mars has two tiny, irregularly shaped moons, Phobos and Deimos.

URANUS The third-largest planet in diameter, Uranus is composed mainly of rock and icy water, ammonia and methane. It is known to have 27 moons. It is unusual in that its spinning axis is parallel with its orbital plane, often pointing almost directly at the Sun. This may be due to a collision with another large body at some point in its past. Uranus orbits the Sun once every 84.3 years and rotates on its axis once every 17 hours and 14 minutes.

PLUTO

NEPTUNE

URANUS

SATURN

PLUTO Smaller than our own Moon, Pluto is a world of icy methane and water. It has three moons: Charon, Hydra and Nix. largest of these, Charon, has a diameter of 593 km. Hydra and were discovered only in 2005. rotates once every 6.4 days and takes 248.1 years to orbit the Unlike the eight planets, Pluto never been visited or closely monitored by a probe from Ear In January 2006, however, NA launched the robotic spacecraf New Horizons, expected to reac Pluto in 2015.

NEPTUNE Although it has a slightly smaller diameter than Uranus, Neptune has a higher density – it is the third most massive body in the Solar System after Jupiter and Saturn. Since Pluto was reclassified, Neptune has once again become the outermost planet in the Solar System. It is known to have 13 moons, but as with most of the outer planets, research into Neptune continues and this list may well be added to in the future. It orbits the Sun once every 165.2 years and rotates on its axis once every 16 hours and 7 minutes.

SATURN With a diameter of 119 900 km and a volume 755 times that of Earth, Saturn is the second-largest planet in the Solar System. Like Jupiter, it is composed mainly of hydrogen and helium. Saturn is famed for its spectacular rings, composed mainly of particles of water ice. Although they are more than 250 000 km in diameter, they are just 1 km thick. Saturn is known to have 47 moons, 35 of which have been named. The largest, Titan, is the second-largest moon of any planet (after Ganymede) and the tenth largest body in the Solar System. Saturn rotates once every 10 hours and 40 minutes and takes 26.7 years to orbit the Sun.

JUPITER This gas giant, made largely of hydrogen and helium, is the Solar System's largest planet, measuring 142 800 km across. In 2003, 23 new moons were discovered, giving it a total of 63. Its four largest – Ganymede, Callisto, Io and Europa, in order of size – are so big that they would be classified as planets if they orbited the Sun rather than Jupiter.

FACTS

ERIS IS THE LARGEST OBJECT IN THE KUIPER BELT.

Slightly larger than Pluto and known to have at least one moon, it was discovered in 2005 and officially designated a dwarf planet in August 2006. It is thought to have a rocky core and an icy surface, and initial calculations suggest that it orbits the Sun once every 556.7 years.

JUPITER closely resembles a star in its composition. If it had been 80 times larger it would have ignited and become a star, forming a binary system with the Sun.

CERES CONTAINS
ABOUT A THIRD OF THE MASS of the Asteroid Belt. Its diameter at its equator is 940 km.

FACTS

EARTH

AS THE SUN FORMED, A DISK-SHAPED CLOUD OF GAS AND DUST WAS LEFT IN SPACE AROUND IT. **The gas condensed around the dust particles and formed larger clumps of matter, much as raindrops form around dust particles in our own atmosphere.** The clumps within the cloud collided and eventually coalesced into planets. One of these was the Earth.

Like all of the planets, the Earth began as a rotating ring in the so-called protoplanetary disk. These rings, which looked rather like the modern rings of Saturn, separated out from one another very early in the Solar

4.6 BILLION YEARS AGO The Earth formed from gas and dust circling the newly burning Sun. As the gas and dust particles collided, they built up into clumps of matter, which were pulled ever closer together by the force of gravity. Slowly, the cloud coalesced into a single protoplanetary mass.

4.6–4.4 BILLION YEARS AGO With the Earth a single sphere, the materials in its interior began to separate out. Gravity pulled the heavy element iron into its centre, where it formed the core. The lighter elements made up the mantle. The Earth was entirely molten, its

EMERGES

System's evolution, leaving vast areas of space between them. Within each rotating ring, collisions and the force of gravity caused most of the planetesimals (see page 22) and other matter to become concentrated around one point. That point became a protoplanet, pulling ever more matter in, the larger it became.

The embryonic Earth formed while the Sun was still small and the Solar System was relatively dark. As the Sun grew and the process of nuclear fusion within it accelerated, it began to generate solar wind. This blasted away most of the gas and other tiny particles that had not yet gathered into larger bodies, scattering them outwards into the vastness of space. What was left were the protoplanets, asteroids and other large bodies.

Molten Earth

At this point, less than 150 million years after the evolution of the Sun and Solar System had begun, the Earth was molten and still accumulating matter. Asteroids and other objects smashed into it and were absorbed. Radioactive material decayed inside it, keeping temperatures high, while heavier elements sank towards the centre as the force of gravity pulled them ever inward. It was at this stage in Earth's history that its layered internal structure was established. At the centre, a core of iron began to form, leaving lighter elements above it to make up the mantle. The

OUR NEAREST NEIGHBOUR

The Moon is probably the result of a collision. Scientists believe that early in the history of the Solar System another, smaller protoplanet, named Theia, formed near the Earth. Dragged by the Earth's gravitation, Theia eventually crashed into it around 4.53 billion years ago. The impact blew parts of the Earth's surface into space, along with parts of Theia. In a short time, perhaps two weeks, the lost matter from the Earth and the remains of Theia coalesced to form the Moon. As a side effect of the collision, the Earth was knocked off its vertical axis, resulting in the tilt that gives us the seasons.

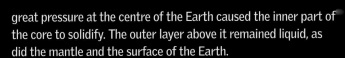

great pressure at the centre of the Earth caused the inner part of the core to solidify. The outer layer above it remained liquid, as did the mantle and the surface of the Earth.

Over the next 100 million years or so, the Earth began to cool. The outer core, with its relatively low melting point, remained liquid but the mantle, composed mainly of silicon-based rocks, began to harden. Although it never became completely solid, the inner part of the mantle turned highly viscous. On the surface of the more liquid outer mantle above it, the first sections of crust began to form – the outer mantle remained less viscous than the inner mantle because it was under less pressure, with less material weighing down on it from above.

Slowly but surely, the sections of crust expanded until, around 4.35 billion years ago, the entire surface of the Earth was covered with a hard, rocky shell. This shell was much more cracked than it is today and there was a great deal more volcanic activity, but the Earth as a planet with a solid surface had finally formed.

4.4–3.8 BILLION YEARS AGO As the Earth cooled, its surface hardened and a crust of solid rock formed. Water brought by comets combined with water forced through the crust by volcanic activity and built up as vapour in the atmosphere. Clouds formed and the first rain fell, creating the seas.

EARTH, FIRE AND WATER

THE EARLY EARTH WAS ALMOST UNRECOGNISABLE AS THE PLANET WE LIVE ON TODAY. Even after its crust had formed, it was a violent and forbidding place. Volcanic eruptions were widespread and lava spilled over the surface. There was no atmosphere to speak of and no surface water. Scientists call this period of the planet's history, before life began, the Hadean eon – after Hades, the ancient Greek vision of Hell. Life could not have begun under these conditions, and even if it had come to Earth from elsewhere, it would have been quickly extinguished. So what changed?

Volcanic eruptions were widespread on the early Earth, and lava spilled over its surface. There was no atmosphere to speak of and no surface water. Scientists call this period of the planet's history, before life began, the Hadean eon – after Hades, the ancient Greek vision of Hell.

The birth of the oceans

The first major step towards the beginning of life was the appearance of the oceans. As the Earth cooled enough for the crust to form, water vapour began to build up along with other gases in what scientists call the Earth's first atmosphere. Every volcanic eruption added to this atmosphere, releasing more and more water vapour and other gases from inside the planet. These were augmented by gases that arrived from space – in its infancy, comets showered the Earth, and much of their payload was ice, which turned to water vapour on impact with the planet.

Gradually, the concentration of water vapour in the atmosphere increased to such an extent that clouds were able to form. The first rain to fall from these almost certainly evaporated before it hit the ground, but eventually the Earth cooled sufficiently for liquid water to pool on its surface. By 4.3 billion years ago, the Earth had oceans beneath its

COMETS
Comets are lumps of matter left over from the creation of the Solar System. Scientists believe that most originate in the Oort Cloud (see page 24), which contains billions of frozen lumps of rock, dust and ice. These become visible as comets if they are pulled from the Oort Cloud into the Solar System – comets from the Oort Cloud pass through the Solar System once and never return, unlike those from the Kuiper Belt. A comet differs from an asteroid or meteoroid by the fact that, when it approaches the Sun, it forms its own atmosphere, called a coma. The Sun's heat melts the comet's outer layers, creating the coma, which consists of dust and gases, including water vapour. A comet also has a tail, which always faces away from the Sun; this is caused by the solar wind blasting off the outer part of the comet's coma. Today, comets are rare and noteworthy events – most stay in the Oort Cloud far beyond the reach of the Sun's gravity. In the Solar System's infancy, they were much more common between and just beyond the planets.

swirling clouds. The land was barren and the atmosphere toxic, but the planet was beginning to take on a familiar face.

To the best of our knowledge, the Earth remained lifeless for another half billion years. It may be that life began and was then wiped out – perhaps more than once – but if this did happen we will probably never know about it. Rocks from that early period are scarce, and forces in the Earth's crust since then have greatly changed most sedimentary rocks (the only ones in which fossils occur) laid down at that time.

Harsh conditions

Conditions on the Earth were still extremely harsh, and they were made worse by events triggered elsewhere in the Solar System. Between around 4.2 and 3.8 billion years ago, the Earth underwent a period when asteroids bombarded it in huge numbers. A shift in the orbit of Jupiter is thought to have caused this – the gravitational effect of the shift hurled rocks out of the Asteroid Belt, which lies beyond Mars (see page 24). The results of this rain of rocks can still be seen on the surface of the Moon – most of its craters were also formed at this time. Doubtless, similar craters then pock-marked the Earth. The fact that they no longer exist is a testament to the dynamic nature of our planet and the immensity of the changes it has undergone since.

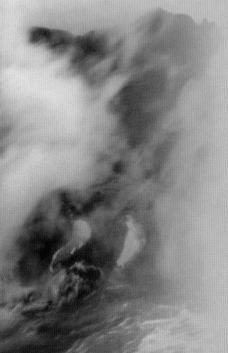

MOLTEN ROCK Lava pours into the sea off Hawaii, creating new land. During Earth's early history, when the crust was still thin, scenes like this would have been common right across the planet.

POWER OF THE SUN

EVEN THOUGH THE SUN LIES MILLIONS OF
KILOMETRES AWAY IN SPACE, IT AFFECTED
VIRTUALLY EVERYTHING IN THE EARLY
EVOLUTION OF THE EARTH, from the formation of
the atmosphere to the appearance of the oceans.
Without it, the Earth as we know it would never have existed.

The Sun reached its present size and brightness while the Earth was still molten.
Then, as now, the Sun emitted a powerful solar wind, a continuous stream of charged
particles that radiate out from it at an incredible speed. This solar wind buffeted the
early planet, driving off its simple, embryonic atmosphere of hydrogen and helium.
The wind was deflected only after the Earth's iron core formed and the planet
developed a protective magnetic field, generated by convection currents in its liquid
outer core. By this time, with the crust forming, there was no atmosphere at all.

The appearance of the magnetic field was a key factor in the development of
the Earth's second, more complex atmosphere. With the magnetic field acting as an
invisible barrier to the solar wind, gases released from the Earth remained around it, held
in place by gravity. These gases, belched out by volcanic activity in the Earth's crust as it

cooled, consisted mainly of water vapour, carbon dioxide, carbon monoxide and sulphur dioxide, along with smaller amounts of methane, ammonia, chlorine and hydrogen. Comets brought other gases to the planet, including water vapour.

Gas build-up

This second atmosphere started building up not long after the creation of the crust. Over a relatively short period, possibly just a few million years, the amount of gas surrounding the planet grew by an incredible amount. At its peak, it is thought that the atmosphere contained around 100 times more gas than there is in our atmosphere today. The predominance of carbon dioxide contributed to a massive greenhouse effect, trapping heat reaching the Earth from the Sun. Even after the crust had almost completely cooled, air temperatures hovered at around 70°C.

Although temperatures were high, they were low enough for water vapour in the atmosphere to condense into clouds and fall as rain on the surface of the planet. Gradually, the amount of water on the surface built up until the pools were large enough to be recognised as the beginnings of the oceans. With much of its water vapour now liquid, the amount of gas in the atmosphere decreased. Most of the carbon dioxide became dissolved in the seas and reacted with other elements to form solid carbonates.

As the decrease in gases continued, the greenhouse effect also lessened, and the temperature around the planet dropped.

While this was happening, the Sun's influence continued. Its rays drove evaporation from the planet's surface and the formation of new clouds and rain. Where this rain fell over land, it washed away surface dust and began the process of erosion. Streams and rivers formed which, over time, carved out valleys and canyons. Lakes appeared in the hollows where water could not escape to the sea. The power of the Sun also created winds. Where its rays struck land, they warmed it up, causing the atmosphere in contact with it to rise. The resulting low atmospheric pressure near the surface was equalised as new atmospheric currents were drawn in. The Sun continues to drive this process of wind creation – and most of the world's weather.

Familiar face

By around 4 billion years ago, the Earth had oceans and weather systems that would not look unfamiliar to us today, but one thing was still missing – life. The atmosphere surrounding the Earth was still toxic, and the Sun was bathing the planet with more than just heat. With no ozone layer to protect it, the land was bombarded with ultraviolet radiation. Although it may have looked benign, the Earth's surface was still as hostile as it had ever been.

SOLAR POWER By driving weather and hence erosion, the Sun shaped the surface of the young Earth just as it does today, as here in California's Yosemite Valley.

THE STAGE IS SET

FOUR BILLION YEARS AGO, THE EARTH WAS BARREN. It had oceans and an atmosphere – but no life and no breathable air. Out of the oceans, conditions on the planet were extremely hostile. Toxic gases filled the air and the land sizzled beneath the Sun's ultraviolet glare. In the oceans, however, conditions were stable. The water acted as an ultraviolet filter, blocking out the radiation. Here, all of the basic ingredients for life were available: water, a host of simple organic (carbon-based) chemicals and possibly some more complex organic molecules. All that was needed was the spark to combine them.

Life on Mars?

But what of the other planets in the Solar System? Could life have emerged on any of them? The best candidate is Mars, where scientists believe that conditions could have been similar to those on the Earth. The evidence comes from features still visible on its surface today. The northern hemisphere of Mars is dotted with gigantic volcanoes, while elsewhere are the remains of smaller volcanic craters. Some have been damaged by asteroid impacts around 4.2 to 3.8 billion years ago, which proves that Mars was volcanically active 4 billion years ago. Mars also has rift valleys. On Earth, these are formed by movements between the plates that make up the crust, suggesting that Mars, too, has a relatively thin crust made up of tectonic plates. At the same time, channels on the surface of Mars indicate that water once flowed on it.

The combination of volcanic activity, plate tectonics and water is associated on Earth with hydrothermal vents, which are known to be favourable places for life (see page 41). There must have been similar vents on Mars, and life could have evolved there, although it seems unlikely that it would have lasted for long. Mars has undergone greater changes than Earth. Its once rich atmosphere has almost completely gone, and temperatures on the surface have plummeted, today averaging around −60°C at its equator. It is just possible that extremely hardy microbes may survive beneath Mars's surface, as they do in the rocks beneath the ocean floor on Earth, but no evidence for this has yet been found.

Water for life

The current theories about how life comes into existence all have one thing in common – they require liquid water to work. This makes it unlikely that life emerged on planets other than Earth and possibly Mars. Venus is surrounded by a thick atmosphere of carbon dioxide, which traps heat. Its average surface temperature is currently 480°C and was probably always too high for liquid water to form. Mercury rotates once every six months or so and sees huge variations in surface temperature. If life ever arose there, it would have been extinguished within a matter of weeks as the planet turned to face the Sun. All of the other planets are too cold for life to have arisen, and scientists believe they were always so.

The only other place in the Solar System where life might have got going, apart from Earth and Mars, is Titan, Saturn's

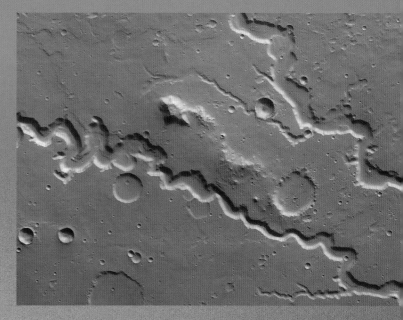

EXTRATERRESTRIAL RIVERS The surface of Mars is covered with snaking channels like these. Most scientists believe that they were carved by running water.

largest moon. Titan is larger than Mercury and is thought to have a hot core. Its atmosphere is rich in nitrogen and contains traces of methane and other organic molecules. Today, Titan's surface is too cold to support liquid water, but this may not always have been the case. If life did arise there, it may still exist in the layer of liquid water thought to lie beneath its crust.

PRIMEVAL SCENE California's Mono Lake, dotted with islands of jagged tufa (calcium carbonate), shows how the Earth might have appeared in the barren days before life began.

THE COM
OF LIFE

ING 2

LIFE ITSELF IS ONE OF NATURE'S GREATEST FORCES OF CHANGE. By definition, living things change over time, and they often change the environment around them. Without life our planet would be unrecognisable, and indeed the appearance of life changed it utterly. Life permanently altered the atmosphere as organisms filled the seas and, later, clothed the land. Today, life occurs in many forms, some of great complexity and beauty. Yet, for a large part of the Earth's history, all living things remained simple. Most were microscopic, but a few gathered in such numbers that they changed the appearance of the places in which they lived, as bacteria do in Yellowstone's hot springs today (left). Here, billions of pigment-bearing, thermophilic (heat-loving) microbes give the often boiling waters their characteristic bright colours.

WHAT IS LIFE?

MOST PEOPLE CAN DISTINGUISH LIVING THINGS FROM NON-LIVING ONES. And yet, although we seem to know instinctively what life is, we still have some difficulty in defining it. One very broad definition is to say that life is a force that both organises and animates matter. It is not a force that can be measured or mathematically described, but it can be observed in action.

Scientists define life by the qualities it requires in order to exist. All living things have certain features in common, and while many things possess some of those characteristics, only those that possess all of them can be regarded as alive. Living things are generally accepted to have seven defining features: they are composed of cells; they use energy; they regulate their internal environment; they grow; they are able to adapt to change; they respond to external stimuli; and they reproduce. The last of the features can be applied accurately only to populations of living organisms: some individuals within a population may be sterile – worker bees, for example – but they are still alive.

Living things are generally accepted to have seven defining features: they are composed of cells; they use energy; they regulate their internal environment; they grow, they are able to adapt to change; they respond to external stimuli; and they reproduce.

MINERAL GROWTH Despite the fact that they may be 'grown', crystals do not possess all the defining features of life and are therefore classified as non-living things.

The membrane barrier

The first defining feature, cellular structure, is vital for life to be maintained. In essence, a living cell is a capsule. All cells – even the simplest, such as those of bacteria – have a membrane that acts as a barrier between the contents of the cell and the world outside. This membrane is the most fundamental of the cell's basic components, and its underlying structure is provided by a layer of fats, called lipids, two molecules thick – the lipid bilayer.

Most cell membranes contain other substances as well, but the lipid bilayer is the key component – so much so that scientists believe that lipids must have existed on the early Earth in order for life to have started in the first place. Other fundamental molecules present in all living things include proteins, made up, in turn, of amino acids, which must also have predated the existence of life on Earth.

While membranes are essential to cellular life, so is genetic material, the molecular code book that directs the activities of living things. Among organisms alive today, most genetic material is made up of DNA (deoxyribonucleic acid).

Growth and reproduction

Life is contained within an organism, but the energy for life to continue comes from outside it. Some organisms, such as amoebas, engulf others in order to obtain energy; some, such as plants, get their energy from the Sun; a few, such as certain bacteria, are able to break down inorganic compounds to release the energy held within them.

All living things use the energy they obtain to drive processes that create more living matter, either through growth or reproduction. Growth is defined as the increase in size of an organism, and reproduction as the creation of a new life or new lives. Single-celled organisms reproduce by splitting in two. Some multicellular organisms are also able to reproduce in this way – certain flatworms, for example – but most reproduce sexually. They generate individual male or female cells, which have the sole purpose of combining in order for new life to begin.

An exception to the rule?

One problem with the definition of life by its seven common features is that it answers some questions but raises others. For example, if all life is cellular, are viruses alive? Viruses are not cellular. They are more simple in structure than even the most primitive bacteria. Yet they display most of the other features of living things. They use energy to reproduce, they can adapt to change and they contain simple genetic material.

Most scientists hold that viruses are not truly alive. While viruses may have originated as living organisms, they are now incapable of reproducing by themselves. The only way they can reproduce is by entering the cells of living organisms and, essentially, hijacking their equipment. The newly formed viruses leave their host cell and immediately become inert. They are only re-animated when they come into contact with another cell, which they enter and use to reproduce again.

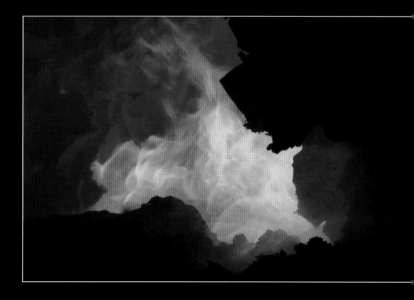

HOW LIFE STARTED

HOW LIFE FIRST STARTED IS A QUESTION THAT HAS LONG PUZZLED SCIENTISTS, AND EVEN TODAY THEY HAVE NO DEFINITIVE ANSWER. Clues do exist, however, and scientists have used these to put forward a number of theories about the origins of life. One clue is provided by certain fundamental molecules, including lipids and amino acids, which are present in all living things.

In 1953, two American scientists, Stanley Miller and Harold Urey, performed an experiment at the University of Chicago, which shed a fascinating light on how these molecules might have come into being. It involved passing an electrical charge through a mixture of three gases – methane, ammonia and hydrogen – thought to have been present in the Earth's atmosphere about the time that life on the planet began. It showed that certain simple organic molecules, such as fatty acids (which make up lipids) and amino acids, can be produced from a mixture of the molecules in the three gases.

Other scientists have since carried out similar experiments using different concentrations of these gases, as well as others believed to have been present in the

Certain simple organic molecules, such as fatty acids and amino acids, can be produced from a mixture of the molecules thought to have been present in the gases in the Earth's atmosphere around the time that life began.

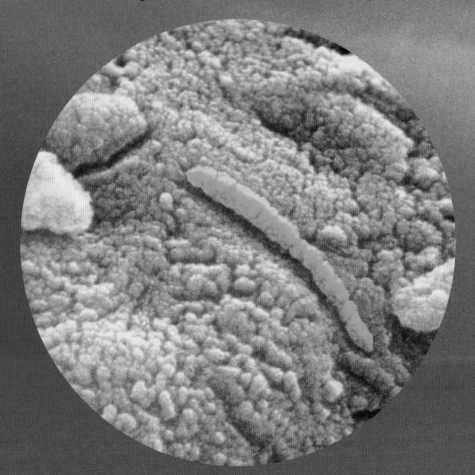

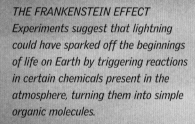

THE FRANKENSTEIN EFFECT Experiments suggest that lightning could have sparked off the beginnings of life on Earth by triggering reactions in certain chemicals present in the atmosphere, turning them into simple organic molecules.

LIFE FROM MARS? Microscopic in size and billions of years old, this tube-like object was found on a meteorite from Mars discovered in Antarctica in 1984. Some believe it could be a fossil and provide evidence that life has existed on the red planet. It may seem fanciful to look to space for the origins of life on Earth, but it is a possible hypothesis.

BLACK SMOKER Some scientists propose that life begin deep in the ocean, in the superheated waters around hydrothermal vents. Here in the darkness there can be no photosynthesis, yet microbes exist, obtaining energy from minerals in the super-heated water.

early atmosphere, and all have yielded similar results. They suggest that every time lightning flashed across the sky in that far distant time, simple organic molecules could have been created from chemicals already in the atmosphere. These molecules would have found their way into the sea via rainfall, building up to form a 'prebiotic soup', from which life could eventually have emerged.

Bubble Theory

The next stage in the development of life – the creation of more complex organic molecules and primitive cells – is less clear. One of the more plausible theories is the Bubble Theory, which suggests how the first cell membranes may have formed. Between 4 billion and 3.8 billion years ago, the oceans are thought to have been rich in phospholipids. These simple lipids, a component in all living cell membranes today, are formed from fatty acids, phosphates and another naturally occurring chemical, usually glycerol.

The Bubble Theory proposes that wave action concentrated phospholipids in shallow waters near the seashore, where the molecules, being hydrophilic (attracted to water) at one end and hydrophobic (repelled by water) at the other, would have spontaneously formed themselves into layers. In the foam

generated by crashing waves, these lipid layers would then have become wrapped around tiny bubbles, and where those bubbles contained water, lipid bilayers would have formed.

Scientists have also put forward a theory about how genetic material might have come into being. Today, most genetic material in living organisms is made up of DNA (deoxyribonucleic acid), but DNA had a more simple precursor in RNA (ribonucleic acid). This is a naturally self-replicating molecule, and scientists think that RNA could have formed spontaneously from its components, including phosphoric acid and ribose (a sugar), under the conditions prevalent on Earth before life began.

Exactly how RNA, lipid bilayers and other materials needed to make the precursors to living cells came together remains a mystery. And unless the process is repeated in a laboratory at some point in the future, it will probably remain so. No one has found any undisturbed sedimentary rock (the only type of rock that contains fossils or other artefacts of life) from that very early period in the Earth's history and probably never will.

Extraterrestrial possibilities

Various other explanations have been put forward to explain how life arose on Earth. One is that it started around deep sea hydrothermal vents (see page 41); another is that life could have come from beyond the Earth – for example, Mars. Life may have arisen on Mars (see page 32), and chunks of rock blasted from its surface by asteroid impacts may have carried organisms to our planet. Martian meteorites have been found on Earth and some contain structures that may have been formed by living things. It has also been suggested that the components of life – but not life itself – may have come to Earth on comets. Organic compounds are believed to be relatively common in the outer Solar System, and early in its history the Earth was bombarded by comets that had passed through this region.

THE FIRST LIFE FORMS

All of the first organisms were prokaryotic – made up of cells without a nucleus. The vast majority lived alone as single cells.

SCIENTISTS BELIEVE THAT LIFE FIRST APPEARED ON EARTH AROUND 3.8 BILLION YEARS AGO. By 3.2 billion years ago, single-celled organisms were living in at least three different ways – as cyanobacteria that captured energy from the Sun for photosynthesis, as bacteria that digested minerals from rocks and as bacteria that absorbed minerals from the water around hydrothermal vents in the sea floor. Descendants of these organisms still exist virtually unchanged, although now they are usually overlooked, hidden by the wealth of larger, more obvious life forms. Yet for millions of years they were the main forms of life on the planet. All of these first organisms were prokaryotic – made up of cells without a nucleus. The vast majority lived alone as single cells. Even those that formed colonies were simply masses of single-celled organisms gathered together.

The oldest fossils

A lack of fossil evidence means that no one is certain which of the three forms of life appeared first. But non-fossil clues in the rocks tell us clearly that life did exist well before the oldest known fossils, which date from just over 3.5 billion years ago. The most important of these clues is the presence of forms of carbon that are known to appear only in living organisms.

The cyanobacteria are the most familiar of the three ancient groups. Sometimes called blue-green algae – misleadingly, because they are not algae at all but bacteria – cyanobacteria use photosynthesis to capture energy from the Sun to create their food. Today, they exist in aquatic environments all over the world – most are single-celled and microscopic. Cyanobacteria formed the world's oldest fossils, but that does not necessarily mean that they were the first life forms. Most known fossils of cyanobacteria are of colonies, and being large, they are easy to find. The other two groups of early life did not form colonies, so evidence for their existence has to come from traces they left behind.

Evidence of the second group – bacteria that digest minerals from rock – came in 2004, when scientists from the University of Bergen in Norway announced that they had discovered microscopic tunnels in 3.5-billion-year-old lavas from South Africa. These tiny tunnels contained high levels of carbon and had been dug by bacteria that lived by digesting minerals in the glassy rind formed

AT THE MARGIN The edge of a thermal pool in New Zealand is thick with micro-organisms (left). The blue-green areas are algae and cyanobacteria.

SOME LIKE IT HOT This thermophilic bacterium (below), magnified about 10 000 times, lives at temperatures of 83°C near underwater hydrothermal vents.

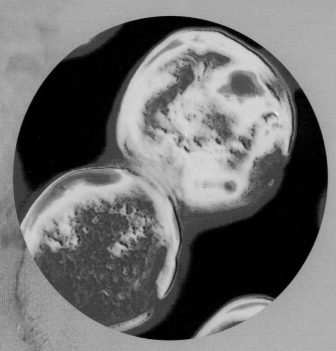

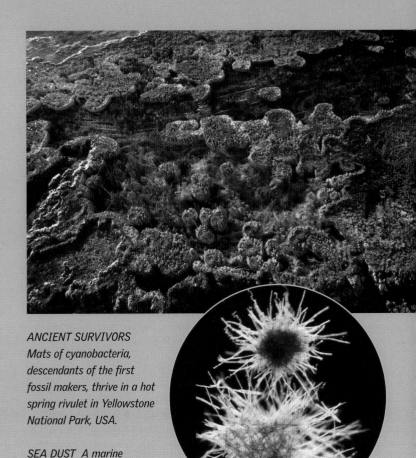

ANCIENT SURVIVORS Mats of cyanobacteria, descendants of the first fossil makers, thrive in a hot spring rivulet in Yellowstone National Park, USA.

SEA DUST A marine cyanobacterium, Trichodesmium, can gather in blooms so vast that they are visible from space.

on the outer surface of the rocks. There are bacteria that live in that way today, and similar microtunnels have been found in recently formed lavas. Upon closer examination these have been shown to contain nucleic acids and high levels of carbon and nitrogen, a combination that is the unmistakable signature of life. Although no one has actually seen the bacteria, the evidence for their existence is overwhelming. Other bacteria that live by digesting minerals in rocks are well known.

Life around black smokers

The third group of ancient organisms for which we have evidence lived around hydrothermal vents on the sea floor. Since modern hydrothermal vents, or 'black smokers', were first discovered on the floor of the eastern Pacfic Ocean in 1977, they have been intensely scrutinised. They are known to support whole communities of organisms that, ultimately, obtain all of their energy from the vents.

Some scientists have even suggested that such vents may have been the original cradle of life – an alternative argument to the more commonly held 'primordial soup' theory. The evidence of early life in such places takes the form of thread-like filaments etched in rocks formed around vents 3.2 billion years ago. Most scientists agree that these filaments almost certainly had a biological origin, although the exact type of micro-organisms that created them remains unknown for now.

HARVESTING SUNLIGHT

THE ARRIVAL OF LIFE ON OUR PLANET BROUGHT ABOUT IMMENSE CHANGES, AND ONE OF THE FIRST THINGS IT ALTERED WAS THE ATMOSPHERE. When life began, there was no oxygen in the air at all; nor was there oxygen dissolved in the oceans. The atmosphere was composed chiefly of carbon dioxide laced with hydrogen sulphide, a cocktail poisonous to modern aerobic (oxygen-requiring) organisms.

Early life forms thrived in this environment, and to this day many of the most primitive bacteria still find oxygen toxic – they die if they are exposed to anything more than the most minute quantities. Nowadays, these organisms are found only in anaerobic (oxygen-free) environments, such as the thick sludge on the seabed. But in the Earth's early history they were probably the most common life forms on the planet.

Photosynthesis takes off

The build-up of oxygen in the atmosphere and oceans was gradual but relentless, driven by photosynthesis. This is a chemical process carried out by some living organisms – notably plants, but also cyanobacteria – to generate food. In photosynthesis, water and carbon dioxide combine to form glucose, a simple carbohydrate. The reaction is driven by energy obtained from sunlight. Oxygen is also created by the process and released as a by-product.

For at least 1.5 billion years, cyanobacteria were the only photosynthesising organisms on the planet. Then, around 2 billion years ago, they were joined by a new group, the single-celled algae. These were among the first eukaryotes – organisms with a cell nucleus – but they were not the first eukaryotes of all. They evolved from another ancestral eukaryote, which at some stage had engulfed some cyanobacteria. Over time, a symbiotic relationship built up between the ancestral eukaryotes and the cyanobacteria inside them. The cyanobacteria were protected by the host cell, and in return the host gained some of the food the cyanobacteria generated. In due course, the cyanobacteria became an integral part of the host – the cell structures we know as chloroplasts. These are the chlorophyll-carrying organelles (specialised structures within a cell) in which photosynthesis takes place in modern algae and plants.

This evolutionary step might sound like speculation, but there is a huge amount of material to back it up – it is as close to a certainty as evolutionary science can get. The most convincing piece of evidence for the development involves DNA. In a eukaryote, the nucleus is the organelle where most of the cell's genetic material is found. But the DNA inside the nucleus of an algal or plant cell does not have the key genes required to encode many of the proteins that make up the cell's chloroplasts. Instead, these genes and others are found inside the chloroplasts themselves, suggesting that they have an independent evolutionary family tree. On top of that, the genetic material carried inside chloroplasts resembles that of cyanobacteria and is very different from that in the algal or plant cell's nucleus.

The ozone layer

With single-celled algae as well as cyanobacteria now filling the oceans, the amount of oxygen in the atmosphere soared. In the stratosphere (the layer of the atmosphere from about 8 km to 50 km above the Earth's surface), some of it turned to ozone. With the chemical formula O_3, ozone is a triatomic form of molecular oxygen (O_2), the gas we refer to simply as 'oxygen'. Ultraviolet light striking the atmosphere split O_2 molecules in two; each of the atoms produced then joined with another O_2 molecule to form O_3. Eventually, this ozone built up into a layer that protected the air and the surface of the Earth below it from the worst of the Sun's ultraviolet rays.

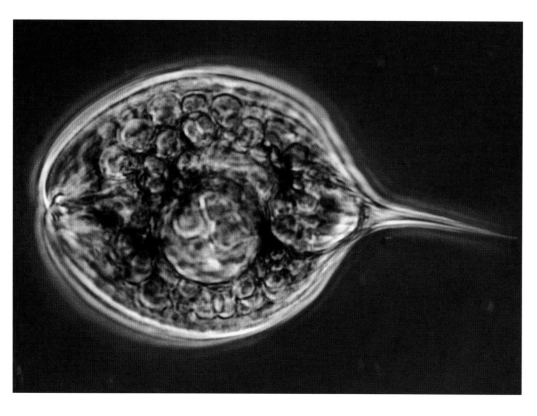

FOOD FACTORY A single-celled aquatic alga of the genus Phacus *has green disk-shaped photosynthesising chloroplasts and is drawn to sunlight, its fuel source, by a light-sensitive organ.*

STROMATOLITES

THE WORLD'S OLDEST FOSSILS ARE OF THICK MATS OF CYANOBACTERIA CALLED STROMATOLITES.

Until 1954, they were known only as fossils, the oldest examples dating to more than 3.5 billion years ago. Then scientists found living stromatolites in the warm, shallow waters of Shark Bay, Western Australia; they have since been discovered elsewhere. Today, these 'living fossils' are rare, but their abundance in early rocks suggests that they once existed all over the Earth, forming a variety of different shapes, including domed structures like the modern ones at Shark Bay. Their variety and abundance declined sharply with the arrival of new life forms, and nowadays stromatolites grow only where creatures that might feed on them are absent.

They form because the cyanobacteria mats secrete a sticky mucus that traps fine particles of sediment suspended in the water. Calcium carbonate cements the particles together, forming a layer. While this is happening, some of the cyanobacteria migrate upwards, closer to the light. They multiply, forming a new mat, which forms a new layer, and so the process continues.

VITAL STATISTICS

DOMAIN: Bacteria
PHYLUM: Cyanobacteria
PERIOD OF EXISTENCE: Around 3.5 billion years ago to the present
GROWTH RATE: 0.04–1 mm per year
ENVIRONMENT: Aquatic, usually hypersaline
MAXIMUM DEPTH: 3.5 m

FROM ONE CELL TO MANY

FOR NEARLY 3 BILLION YEARS – IN OTHER WORDS, FOR MOST OF THE EARTH'S HISTORY – SINGLE-CELLED ORGANISMS WERE THE ONLY LIFE FORMS. All of these organisms would have been invisible to the naked eye, except when they formed colonies. Then, some time between a billion and 720 million billion years ago, multicellular life appeared. To put this timetable into perspective, if the history of the world was compressed into a single day, life appeared at around ten past four in the morning and remained single-celled until around eight in the evening.

Multicellular life evolved from among single-celled organisms, called eukaryotes, that had a nucleus and other cell bodies; organisms without a nucleus – the bacteria and their allies – never evolved into multicellular forms. By the time the eukaryotes took this evolutionary step, they had existed in the oceans for more than a billion years. Single-celled eukaryotes continue to survive today – amoebas are examples, as are single-celled algae.

The drive to evolution

Scientists believe that multicelled organisms evolved more than once. In fact, most think that they evolved at least 16 different times, so rather than having the same multicellular ancestor, animals, land plants, fungi and other forms of life trace their family trees back to different ancestral organisms.

If the history of the world was compressed into a single day, life appeared at around ten past four in the morning and remained single-celled until around eight in the evening.

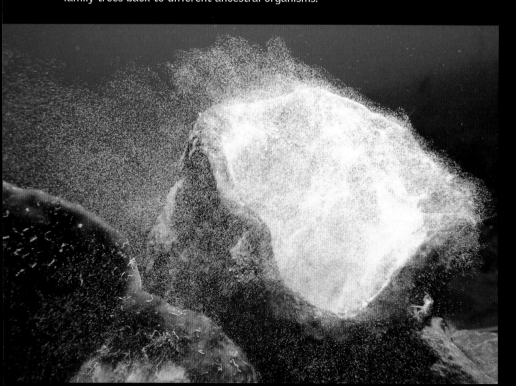

FIRST OF MANY? The simplest of modern animals, sponges (left) share characteristics with a group of single-celled organisms called choanoflagellates. Scientists believe that the choanoflagellates may provide the link between single-celled organisms and multicellular animals.

EXPLOSION OF LIFE Once multicellular organisms had evolved, life diversified relatively quickly, though it was still confined to the oceans. Animals, including sea anemones and ancestral starfish, arrived on the scene between 542 and 505 million years ago.

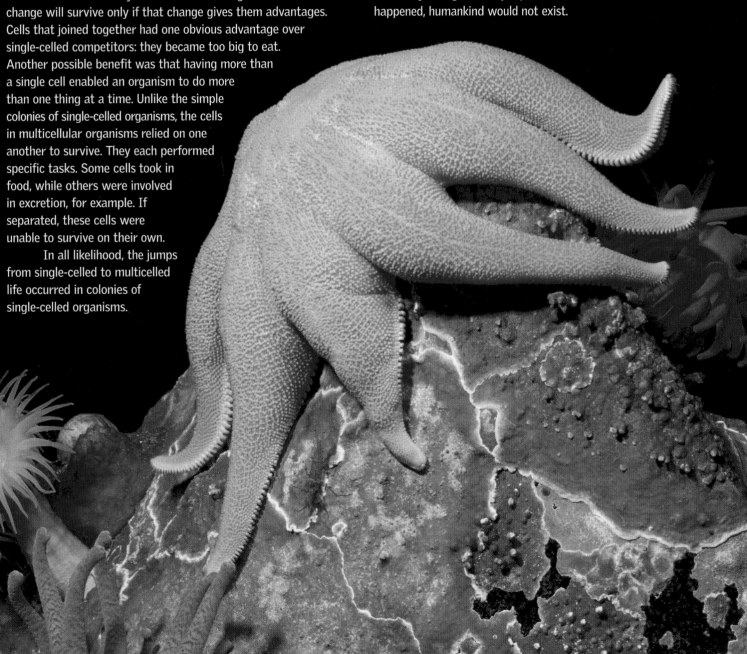

DADDY OF THEM ALL Sunlight suffuses through giant kelp off California. Modern seaweeds are multicellular algae, the direct descendants of the first multicelled organisms.

The individuals within the colony became increasingly specialised and increasingly reliant on one another until they became one multicelled organism. The first multicellular organisms are thought to have been algae, the ancestors of modern seaweeds.

A giant leap

The appearance of multicellular organisms marked the beginning of a new chapter in the story of life on Earth, although it was far from the end for single-celled life. Even today, single-celled organisms massively outnumber multicellular ones. As far as we are concerned, though, it was a key change. If the jump to multicellular life had never happened, humankind would not exist.

All evolution is driven by natural selection: organisms that change will survive only if that change gives them advantages. Cells that joined together had one obvious advantage over single-celled competitors: they became too big to eat. Another possible benefit was that having more than a single cell enabled an organism to do more than one thing at a time. Unlike the simple colonies of single-celled organisms, the cells in multicellular organisms relied on one another to survive. They each performed specific tasks. Some cells took in food, while others were involved in excretion, for example. If separated, these cells were unable to survive on their own.

In all likelihood, the jumps from single-celled to multicelled life occurred in colonies of single-celled organisms.

EVOLUTION CHANGES GEAR

THE APPEARANCE OF MULTICELLULAR ORGANISMS LED TO AN EXPLOSION OF NEW LIFE FORMS. While single-celled organisms were many in number, they were not particularly varied. But with different cells now carrying out specialised functions within individual bodies, the way was clear for organisms of all shapes and sizes to develop.

Soon after the first multicellular algae appeared, so did the earliest animal life. Scientists define an animal as a multicellular organism that eats organic (living) matter; other kinds of multicellular organisms – plants, for example – create their food from inorganic (non-living) materials or, in the case of fungi, grow through their food. According to recent genetic research, sponges were the first animals and the direct ancestors of all modern animal life. Sponges are extremely simple animals,

ARMS RACE The nautilus is related to squids. It is about 25 cm across and has a coiled shell, but much larger, now extinct, ancestors of this creature were the top predators in the early seas.

made up of just a few types of cell, which live by filtering seawater to sieve out tiny particles of food. They have a unique ability that may give an insight into how multicellular life forms evolved. If you took a sponge to pieces, right down to cell level, it would put itself back together again. In addition, if you mixed in cells from another sponge species during the operation, the various cells would join up only with others of their own type.

Mysterious beings

Discounting algae, the earliest fossils of multicellular life forms are around 600 million years old. They consist of circular impressions made by simple cup-shaped organisms and were discovered in the Mackenzie Mountains in north-western Canada. These fossils cannot be algae because the rocks in which they were found were originally formed on the deep sea floor, far from light. Perhaps they were early animals; perhaps they belonged to another group of life forms that has long been extinct – no one knows. Fossil evidence for sponges living at this time does not exist, but that does not

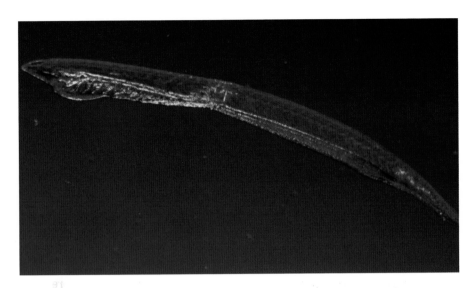

FISH FORERUNNER The lancelet, a small fish-like animal, may resemble the ancestor of the vertebrates, including ourselves. This is a lancelet larva, an immature tadpole-like stage.

mean that they were not around. Fossil-bearing rocks dating from 600 million years ago are rare, and most sponges, being soft-bodied, do not fossilise well.

Life diversifies

The immense stretch of time from the Earth's formation to 542 million years ago is called the Precambrian. Although animals appeared towards the very end of this time, fossil evidence for them is slim. In the succeeding Cambrian period, evidence becomes solid and plentiful.

The Cambrian period lasted from 542 to 505 million years ago and saw the rise of a huge variety of life forms. Moreover, many of the fossils from this period are of creatures that resemble animals alive today. Such modern creatures include brachiopods, shellfish that mostly live in cold water and look like clams, although they are not closely related to them. There are also Cambrian fossils of cnidarians – today's jellyfish and sea anemones – as well as of ancestral starfishes and many different worms. Cambrian rocks contain the earliest fossils of sclerosponges – sponges that consist of soft tissue surrounding a skeleton of calcium carbonate. Also called coralline sponges, they still exist and can live for up to 1000 years. Because of this longevity, they are useful to climatologists, who study their skeletons to determine how water conditions have altered over time.

Arthropods also appeared during the Cambrian. This grouping of animals makes up more than 75 per cent of all known animal species on Earth, both living and fossil. The arthropod grouping includes all insects and spiders, centipedes and millipedes, crabs and lobsters. It also includes the trilobites, hard-shelled creatures ranging from under 1 mm to 70 cm in length. Around 17 000 species are known to have existed. All had gone extinct by about 250 million years ago, but their fossils are widespread and familiar.

Rise of the chordates

Another group of life forms that first appeared during the Cambrian was the chordates. Named for the nerve cord that all of them have at some stage in their lives, the chordates today include the vertebrates (animals with backbones) and hence humankind. The Cambrian chordates, the forerunners of modern sea squirts and lancelets, had soft bodies and the beginnings of a nervous system not unlike our own.

It was from the early chordates that the first fish evolved some time around 470 million years ago. Early fish were jawless and looked rather bizarre. Most had heavy body armour instead of scales, probably to protect them from the superpredators of the time, also found in the fossil record – large, shelled squid-like creatures that could grow up to 10 m long. The first fish with true jaws were the ancestors of the sharks, which began to appear in the oceans around 450 million years ago. Within a further 50 million years, sharks very like those we know today were swimming in the seas.

FOSSIL ROCK

Many types of sedimentary rock contain fossils, but there is one that is formed from fossils and nothing else – chalk. Chalk is a limestone made up from the microscopic remains of single-celled marine algae (below). As these algae died, their tiny bodies sank and everything apart from their shells rotted away. Over millions of years, these accumulated into thick layers that became compressed to form chalk rock. Shelly limestones are another type of limestone with a biological origin, made up mainly of sea shells, as their name suggests, or occasionally fragments of coral. Both chalk and shelly limestones are still being laid down in the oceans as the processes behind their formation continue today.

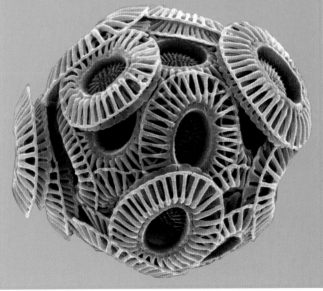

INVADING THE LAND

THE LAND ON EARTH REMAINED BARREN LONG AFTER LIFE WAS FLOURISHING IN THE OCEANS. The main obstacle to terrestrial life was the Sun's ultraviolet radiation, which continued to bombard the face of the Earth as the atmosphere formed. Water provided an effective shield against the deadly rays, soaking them up before they could penetrate much below the surface. Although it seems likely that life moved from the seas into and up the deeper rivers, nothing survived on their banks.

Gradually, conditions changed. Oxygen slowly built up in the atmosphere, and in the stratosphere the ozone layer grew. Eventually, it became thick enough to block the worst of the Sun's glare, reducing the amount of ultraviolet radiation that reached the land below. Conditions became ripe for life to move in.

The first colonisers were probably bacteria and other micro-organisms, although no fossils of these creatures remain as proof. Initially, they would have stayed close to water, moving into the gaps between sand grains and the cracks between rocks – places that were slightly shielded from the Sun. Then, as the ozone layer thickened, they would have moved out onto the surface of the land itself. Multiplying within the early sediments, they would have added their tiny bodies to the mixture, forming the very first simple soils.

FIRST GREEN FINGERS Liverworts are the descendants of the first plants to colonise the land. Their importance cannot be overstated: without terrestrial plants on which to feed, animal life could never have left the water.

ANCIENT HUNTER Multiple-legged invertebrates, such as millipedes and centipedes, were among the first animals to venture onto land. Modern millipedes and centipedes can reach lengths of 30 cm or more. An ancient variety – Arthropleura – could be up to 2 m long.

onto land. Indeed, the oldest known true scorpion, an aquatic creature called *Proscorpius*, was virtually indistinguishable from the land scorpions alive today. *Proscorpius* lived 420 million years ago and was about 3.5 cm long, with walking legs, pincers and a sting mounted on a flexible tail.

Insects appear

The earliest insect fossil – also discovered in Scotland – dates from 400 million years ago. Until recently it was thought that insects, the largest grouping of arthropods, first appeared around that time, with winged insects following on around 70 million years later. In 2004, however, a study of that early fossil was published, which caused scientists to revise their theories. It revealed that the relationship between the fossil and winged insects was closer than had previously been realised and that flight probably developed earlier than had been thought.

In fact, insects probably first appeared on Earth more than 430 million years ago and were among the first land animals. Finding older fossils would help prove this theory, but such a discovery is unlikely because insects do not fossilise well in rock. The most complete insect remains are preserved in amber – resin that leaked from trees, and then engulfed creatures, before hardening and eventually fossilising. But since resin-bearing trees did not appear until 360 million years ago at the earliest, rock fossils are all we can hope for.

So far no one knows exactly when all this happened. We do know from fossils that plants had started to colonise the land by 475 million years ago at the latest, but the process may well have started even further back than that. Despite the lack of earlier plant fossils, studies of genetic material suggest that land plants may date back as far as 700 million years ago and fungi to 1.3 billion years ago.

March of the creepy-crawlies

With the land slowly growing a carpet of green, animals began to emerge from the water. The first wave of creatures were all invertebrates (animals without backbones) and they quickly evolved from water-dwellers into land-living forms. The evidence, including trackways of fossil footprints, points to these earliest land animals being arthropods, possibly millipedes. The oldest known fossil of a land animal is of a millipede; it was found in Scotland in rocks 428 million years old (see box, right). These many-legged creatures still exist today and still eat plants, the only major food source on land in those distant times.

Other animals have been found in fossils that are almost as old. They include centipedes, which are related to the millipedes but differ from them in being venomous predators, and spider-like animals called trigonotarbids, which are now extinct. Logic seems to dictate that these predators evolved after millipedes, but they may not have done; older fossils may be waiting to be found, and these hunters may have originally chased some other, now extinct, vegetarian prey.

Like the trigonotarbids, the scorpions are related to the spiders and form another very early group of land predators. Fossils of scorpions show that they first lived in water and barely changed in appearance when they moved

THE EARLIEST EVIDENCE FOR PLANT LIFE ON LAND

comes from boreholes sunk into the rock beneath the deserts of Oman. In 2003, British and Omani scientists announced the discovery of microscopic fossiled spores along with fragments of the plants that produced them. They dated from 475 million years ago.

THE OLDEST KNOWN FOSSIL

of a land animal is a millipede, discovered by an Aberdeen bus driver and keen amateur fossil hunter, Mike Newman. He found it on the shore near Stonehaven in Scotland in 2001. The 428-million-year-old millipede was named after him: *Pneumodesmus newmani*.

FACTS

OUR ANCESTORS EMERGE

INVERTEBRATES HAD THE LAND TO THEMSELVES FOR AT LEAST 50 MILLION YEARS. Then, around 375 million years ago, fish first hauled themselves from the water. The transition to land is often portrayed as having been a move from the sea, but it is more likely that our vertebrate ancestors emerged from rivers or swamps.

Today, there are many kinds of freshwater fish that can take in air as well as obtain oxygen through their gills. Lungfish, for example, turn to breathing air when their homes disappear because of drought; many other fish gulp air when oxygen levels in the water become too low to survive; and the walking catfish can even travel short distances over land to find a new area of water if its habitat dries up.

The constant threat of drought and the low oxygen levels that occur naturally in many freshwater habitats make it likely that land vertebrates evolved from freshwater, not saltwater, fish. It is a natural progression, since a fish that could breathe air in those situations would have an advantage over one that could not – and such threats do not exist in the sea. The second, perhaps more compelling item of evidence is that the first land vertebrates were amphibians. The vast majority of amphibians spend at least part of their lives in fresh water, but none of them live in the sea. If amphibians become trapped in salt water, they die.

Food – the driving force

Although the evolution of air-breathing fish was probably an adaptation to the perils of living in fresh water, the move to the land was in all likelihood driven by the need for food. The banks and shores of the rivers and lakes in which the first air-breathing fish lived must have been literally crawling with invertebrates. It is not hard to imagine these fish shimmying out onto the land to snap up some prey.

Those that were able to move more easily on land would have had a further advantage over their competitors, driving the evolution of legs. We know that before amphibians appeared

HALFWAY HOUSE Looking at the mudskipper, it is not hard to visualise the scene as vertebrates dragged themselves ashore for the first time. Although they can survive out of water, these fish do not have lungs. They breathe on land through their skin.

there were fish with strong, bony pelvic and pectoral fins, which they used to prop themselves up on the bottom. One group of these were the ancestors of the lungfish, while another, the coelacanths, still survive in the oceans today. So far, no one has found a fossil that links these lobe-finned fish directly to their four-legged descendants. New fossil creatures are discovered almost every week, however, and there are vast areas of potentially fossil-bearing rock yet to be explored. Recent finds of feathered-dinosaur fossils continue to shed light on the connection between dinosaurs and birds, so perhaps the link between fish and amphibians will one day be unearthed.

A slow business

It took millions of years for lobe-finned fish to evolve into true amphibians. The earliest known amphibian, *Elginerpeton*, appeared 368 million years ago, and *Ichthyostega* followed around 5 million years later. Only fossilised fragments of the former have ever been found – parts of the legs, jaw, hip and shoulder – but several almost complete specimens of *Ichthyostega* exist. Both of these animals were quite large, measuring around 1.5 m in length. They probably spent most of

their time in the water, hunting fish and large invertebrates, much as the similarly massive Chinese giant salamander (*Andrias davidianus*) does today. Their young, on the other hand, may well have hunted smaller creatures on land.

Amphibian heyday

Over the next 50 million years, amphibians diversified and spread. Most of the true land-living species were small, equivalent in size to modern lizards. Some of these – the aistopods – lost their legs and became snake-like in appearance, while in other species, such as the metre-long *Dendrerpeton*, the walking limbs strengthened and grew. The largest amphibians were all aquatic. Some may have basked out of water, like modern crocodiles, but all hunted beneath it.

Even the land-living species had to return to the water to breed, like most modern amphibians do. The eggs they laid were soft and their young tadpoles were fish-like and aquatic. The oldest fossils of tadpoles, those of the ancient amphibian *Balanerpeton*, are 338 million years old. Like the tadpoles of modern newts, these youngsters had external gills, which they lost as they grew older.

THE FIRST FORESTS

THE EARLIEST LAND PLANTS WERE SMALL GROUND-HUGGING LIFE FORMS THAT EVOLVED FROM GREEN ALGAE. Their descendants still exist, almost unchanged, today. Known as liverworts, they have flat, almost plate-like bodies (they are not true stems) and live in wet places, such as in moist soil or on damp rocks or on tree trunks.

As a reminder of their aquatic ancestry, liverworts usually require water to reproduce. Some types need to be covered in a continuous film of water so that their sperm (male sex cells) can swim across to the egg (female sex cells). Others use raindrops to disperse their sperm. The male sex cells sit in cup-shaped structures. Any raindrops hitting these structures fragment, and the droplets carry off the sperm, which, hopefully, comes into contact with a female plant nearby. Liverworts can also reproduce asexually (without sex), however, by casting off parts of themselves, which

MIST AND MONSTERS The tree fern forests of the Carboniferous period would have hummed and clicked with the presence of huge dragonflies and millipedes. Fern forests, such as this one on New Zealand's South Island, are still with us, but the monsters have gone.

SET IN STONE Pecopteris polymorpha *was a common type of tree fern in the coal-forming swamps of what is now the United States. Although tree ferns still exist today, they are not closely related to* Pecopteris. *Its descendants do not grow as big.*

then take hold and grow if the conditions are right. Also called vegetative reproduction, this process allows plants, which of course cannot move, to spread when there are no individuals of the opposite sex nearby. When plants first came onto the land, they faced severe difficulties in arranging for their male and female sex cells to meet. This may be why many of them – including trees, such as the ash – can still reproduce asexually.

Moisture lovers

Liverworts were soon followed by another, more familiar, plant group – the mosses. Like the liverworts, early mosses grew close to the ground and thrived only in relatively moist habitats. Unlike liverworts, however, mosses had branched shoots. These branches, although small, enabled the plants to lift their leaves upwards towards the Sun. Over millions of years, competition for light between individual mosses growing close together caused them to develop longer, more upright branches. Eventually these became what we would now recognise as tiny stems.

While these new, upright mosses were evolving, another group of plants appeared. Whereas mosses and liverworts had a very simple construction that relied on water and nutrients moving directly from one cell to the next, the new plants had a more complex internal structure. They contained a system of tubes for transporting water and food from one part of the plant to another, removing the need to grow low to the ground. These were the vascular plants, and today they make up the vast majority of all the plant life on Earth, including the tallest trees. To begin with, however, they were small, not much bigger than the mosses they grew alongside.

Onward and upward

One of the earliest vascular plants was a simple branched organism called *Cooksonia*. It appeared around 425 million years ago and grew to just a few centimetres tall – an insignificant height by modern standards but enough to enable it to compete for light with most mosses. Before long, *Cooksonia* was joined by larger vascular plants. Among the next to appear were the confusingly named club mosses. This group is, in fact, unrelated to the true mosses and its members would soon outstrip them in size. Unlike *Cooksonia*, these plants had true roots, giving them a firm base from which to grow upwards. With their sturdy stems and thick branches, they formed the first-ever bushes and trees.

Club mosses were the dominant plants on land for 50 million years. Then, around 365 million years ago, they were joined by two other groups – the ferns and the horsetails. With the arrival of these new competitors, the race for light stepped up a gear. All three groups developed massive forms. Tree ferns still exist today – as do the club mosses and horsetails, although their giant forms have long since disappeared. Some of these extinct plants were the size of large trees. The giant club moss *Lepidodendron* reached heights of 40 m, while the horsetail *Calamites* grew to 15 m tall.

Coal-bearing forests

These plants formed the forests that covered the Earth when the first amphibians appeared. Although the newly evolved land vertebrates went on to become the most abundant and widespread animals in this often swampy environment, they were not necessarily the largest. In the waters lurked huge predatory fish, such as *Rhizodus hibberti*, which may have been as much as 7 m long, along with giant invertebrates like the 1.5 m long semi-aquatic scorpion *Hibbertopterus*. The forests, too, were filled with an array of invertebrate life unlike anything seen before or since. Giant 2 m long millipedes, such as *Arthropleura*, as well as monstrous 70 cm land scorpions roamed beneath their branches, and dragonflies like *Meganeura*, with the wingspans of seagulls, zipped among their trunks.

These invertebrates were able to grow to such sizes because the Earth's atmosphere contained a third more oxygen than it does today. This was a direct result of the growth of these early forests, which thrived in the relative warmth bathing the Earth at that time, pumping out oxygen while consuming carbon dioxide. The great forests of club mosses, tree ferns and horsetails lasted for more than 70 million years. As their trunks, branches and leaves fell, they became compacted and were gradually buried deeper and deeper. Their remains today make up most of the world's coal beds. Hence the name for this section of Earth's history – the Carboniferous (coal-bearing) period.

LEAVING THE WATER BEHIND

FOR TENS OF MILLIONS OF YEARS, VERTEBRATE LIFE REMAINED TIED TO THE WATER. Amphibians, with their moist skins, required damp habitats. They also needed water in which to reproduce: their soft, shell-less eggs would have dried out on land, and the young also lived in water during the larval (tadpole) stage. For this reason, much of the land was off-limits to vertebrates. Wherever it was dry, insects and their invertebrate allies made up the only animal life.

All of that changed with the first reptiles. They had stronger jaws and legs than amphibians did, but the most important difference was that, unlike amphibians, they had dry, scaly skins and produced eggs with tough shells that they laid on land. While reptiles thrived in moist forests, they were able to move into dry habitats as well. As they broke this new ground, they evolved into a wide range of forms, and with no vertebrate competitors, they became the top land predators across much of the Earth. Some reptiles evolved into plant-eaters, exploiting a food source that the vast majority of amphibians had ignored.

The first reptiles evolved early in the second half of the Carboniferous period, when the Earth's climate was still fairly warm and most of the land was still covered with thick forest. Just as no one has yet found the animal that connects fish with

The first reptiles evolved early in the second half of the Carboniferous period, when the Earth's climate was still fairly warm and most of the land was still covered with thick forest.

HARD CASE The hard shells of reptile eggs meant that parents did not have to lay in water. This hatchling lace monitor has an extra yolk for initial sustenance.

FROG SPAWN Amphibian eggs, unlike those of reptiles (opposite), are soft and must be laid in water, like the spawn of these frogs. In addition, most amphibians pass through a larval (tadpole) phase, which is also confined to water.

amphibians, so the link between amphibians and reptiles is still unknown. The earliest reptile fossil is of *Hylonomus*, an animal that appeared around 310 million years ago. It hunted insects and other invertebrates and grew to about 20 cm long. Although it looked rather like many modern-day lizards, it was only very distantly related to them.

Reptiles continued to look lizard-like for the remainder of the Carboniferous period, which ended 286 million years ago. During this time, they split into three distinct groups. Although outwardly they looked similar, the groups differed in the way their skeletons formed, most notably their skulls.

A parting of the ways

The first of these groups to appear were the anapsids, which included *Hylonomus*. Anapsid skulls were solid and boxy, like those of the amphibians. Anapsid reptiles still exist today as tortoises and turtles.

The second group were the synapsids. These reptiles differed from the anapsids in having a pair of holes in the skull, one opening behind each eye socket, to which the jaw muscles were attached. The first synapsids were the pelycosaurs, lizard-like animals that may have been warm-blooded – that is, they could heat their bodies from within – unlike the other reptiles, which were cold-blooded and required external warmth.

The earliest known pelycosaur is *Archaeothyris*, a meat-eater that grew to about 50 cm and may have lived alongside, and even eaten, *Hylonomus*. Synapsids used to be called mammal-like reptiles, and mammals did indeed evolve from this group. Synapsids are rather a grey area in evolution, since some scientists do not regard them as reptiles at all.

Dinosaur ancestors

The third group of early reptiles were the diapsids, which had two pairs of jaw muscle openings in the skull. The earliest known diapsid was *Petrolacosaurus*, a 40 cm long insect-eater that lived towards the end of the Carboniferous period, found in what is now Kansas, USA. Most of the reptiles alive today are diapsids. It was this group that would eventually give rise to the dinosaurs and ultimately to their descendants, the birds.

FACTS

THE TEMPERATURE AT WHICH REPTILES INCUBATE AS EGGS can determine their sex. With many reptiles, if a clutch is kept too warm or becomes too cool, all of the hatchlings will be of the same gender.

NOT ALL REPTILES ARE ANCIENT. Snakes, for example, evolved around 150 million years ago, long after the first mammals had appeared on the Earth.

THE EARLIEST FOSSILISED REPTILE EGG IS 220 million years old.

FACTS

A CHANGE OF CLIMATE

AS THE CARBONIFEROUS PERIOD ENDED, EARTH'S HISTORY ENTERED A NEW PHASE. Previously, the planet had two supercontinents – Laurasia in the north and Gondwanaland in the south. Now, these two began to merge, forming a single gigantic land mass called Pangaea. Cut off from the oceans, huge areas of land in the middle of Pangaea dried out.

These drier conditions did not suit the previously diverse amphibians, which became less varied as the moist forests disappeared. In their place was desert and arid scrub, or drier forests dominated by conifers, palm-like cycads and seed ferns – a now extinct fern-like group that comprised the first seed-bearing plants. This is called the Permian period of Earth's history.

EYE ON THE PAST New Zealand's tuataras are the last of a group of lizard-like reptiles that appeared around 225 million years ago. Other members of the group went extinct with the dinosaurs 160 million years later.

Although arid conditions are not good for fossilisation, which tends to begin in sediments under water, several fossil sites have been found that give us a window onto Permian life. The most notable change from the Carboniferous period was the increase in both the number and variety of reptiles on land. Although small, lizard-like creatures still existed, there were now much larger reptiles, too.

The sail-backs

The majority of these big animals were pelycosaurs, the most familiar of which is *Dimetrodon*, a formidable 3 m long creature with a spectacular 'sail' along its back. Supported by bony spines and perhaps covered with tissue laden with blood vessels, this sail may have enabled *Dimetrodon* to warm up by

turning sideways to the Sun and cool down by turning away from it. Alternatively, it may have been a visual signal to scare off rivals or attract a mate. People sometimes mistake *Dimetrodon* for a dinosaur because of its massive head and fearsome slashing teeth, but it was only very distantly related to the dinosaurs, which did not evolve until 40 million years later. *Dimetrodon* was a hunter and almost certainly preyed on *Edaphosaurus*, a sail-backed pelycosaur of a similar size that was one of the first large plant-eating reptiles.

Pelycosaurs were the dominant animal life on the land throughout the early Permian and their remains make up around 70 per cent of all the reptile fossils known from that time. Besides the distinctive *Dimetrodon* and *Edaphosaurus*, the group included the largest reptile of the early Permian and the largest land animal up to that time – *Cotylorhynchus*. Without a sail – like the majority of pelycosaurs – this massive plant-eater was the elephant or rhinoceros of its day, measuring up to 6 m long and weighing around 2 tonnes as an adult.

Moschops and *Gorgonops*

In the second half of the Permian period, a new group of synapsids began to take over from the pelycosaurs as the dominant land animals. These creatures, called therapsids, differed subtly from the pelycosaurs in the arrangement of their skull bones, jaw bones and teeth. The therapsids eventually evolved into mammals, but at this time bore little outward resemblance to them.

Like the pelycosaurs, the therapsids could be flesh-eating or vegetarian. Among the latter type was *Moschops*, a muscular, barrel-shaped animal with short legs and a large head. In some individuals, the top of the skull was a full 10 cm thick, suggesting that the males may have clashed heads in fights for dominance, as rams do today. *Moschops*, which grew to 5 m long, had a full set of chisel-like teeth. Many other plant-eating therapsids, however, were toothless. They used sharp-edged jaws to snip off foliage, like tortoises do today, although a few were also equipped with a pair of short tusks, perhaps to help them to dig for roots and tubers.

The plant-eating therapsids roamed Pangaea in herds and were preyed on by a range of meat-eaters, including the monstrous *Gorgonops*, which reached 4 m from nose to tail. It was armed with dagger-like canines, not unlike those of a sabre-toothed cat.

By water and air

Not all of the late Permian reptiles were giants. Most of the diapsids, for instance, were small, and while the majority were land-dwellers, a few species spent at least some time in the water. The best known of these early semi-aquatic reptiles is *Hovasaurus*. A 50 cm long hunter, *Hovasaurus* powered its way through the water with its long, flattened tail, which was almost twice as long as the rest of its body. It steered with its

SAND DWELLER Australia's thorny devil demonstrates that reptiles can live in the driest conditions. Covered with sharp spines, this 20 cm long lizard feeds on ants in its desert home. Despite its thorny protection, it is itself hunted by larger reptiles and birds of prey.

legs, which were fairly long and powerful and suggest that *Hovasaurus* also had little difficulty moving on land.

Another Permian diapsid, meanwhile, took to the air. *Coelurosauravus*, a small insect-eater, had elongated ribs that protruded from its sides and were connected by membranes of skin. Although it could not actually fly, it was able to extend its ribs outwards to create simple wings and glide from tree to tree. This feature has evolved independently several times since and can be seen in some modern rainforest lizards. *Coelurosauravus* was the first creature in which it appeared and the first-ever vertebrate to share the air with insects.

End of an era

The Permian period saw a burgeoning of new life forms, but it all came to a sudden end around 245 million years ago, when the Earth suffered a mass extinction that marked not only the end of the Permian period but also the end of the Palaeozoic era. Some 90 per cent of species – perhaps even more – are estimated to have vanished. What caused this catastrophe is uncertain, but its effect is written in the rocks. Those laid down before 245 million years ago are rich in fossils; those from the following few million years are virtually empty of signs of life.

Somehow, a few species did survive the extinction, among them representatives of the anapsids, synapsids and diapsids. In time, those survivors went on to evolve new forms, filling the many niches left empty by their vanished kin.

IN THE AGE OF DINOSAURS

HUMAN BEINGS ARE A PART OF NATURE AS MUCH AS ALL OTHER ANIMALS ARE. We are mammals – warm-blooded vertebrates that produce milk – and today our species and other mammals dominate the Earth. But it was not always that way. For more than two-thirds of mammal history, they lived in the shadow of the dinosaurs.

Mammals and dinosaurs both appeared around 230 million years ago, and were competitors in the great evolutionary race to repopulate the planet after the mass extinction at the end of the Permian. The dinosaurs prospered, evolving into a huge range of forms, including the largest land animals that ever lived. Their group dominated the Earth for 165 million years. The mammals came to prominence only after the dinosaurs had gone.

The fact that mammals survived to the present day when dinosaurs died out does not mean that mammals were somehow superior: when both groups were present on the Earth, the dinosaurs dominated completely. Far from being the lumbering, slow-witted creatures they are sometimes portrayed as, dinosaurs were highly evolved.

EGG-LAYING MAMMALS
Along with the echidnas, or spiny anteaters, Australia's duck-billed platypus is the last of the egg-laying monotremes, the oldest surviving group of mammals.

SMALL FRY Early mammals were shrew-like in size and appearance and ate invertebrates, although some also fed on plants. The large tree shrew from South-east Asia has a similar diet and looks rather like many of those early mammals did.

Repenomamus robustus. Besides being larger than others mammals living at that time, *Repenomamus*, which lived 130 million years ago, was a meat-eater – one fossilised example had a baby dinosaur in its stomach.

Today, just three mammal groups exist: the monotremes (the duck-billed platypus and spiny anteaters), marsupials (kangaroos and their relatives) and placental mammals (all other modern mammals). Of these, the monotremes are the oldest, dating back at least 160 million years. Unlike other modern mammals, they lay eggs, as all early mammals probably did. The marsupials and placental mammals evolved around 50 million years later, but as long as dinosaurs roamed the planet, all three groups were trapped in a sort of evolutionary straitjacket, unable to break free from the few restricted niches their ancestors had occupied before them.

Some of the meat-eaters in particular were fast-moving and agile, and several types may have hunted in packs, making them perhaps as intelligent as modern pack-hunters, such as wolves.

While dinosaurs lived, the options for mammals were limited. Most early mammals were invertivores (invertebrate-eaters), living on a diet of insects and worms. This was one niche that dinosaurs never occupied or competed for, leaving it free for mammals to fill. It seems likely that most of these mammals were nocturnal. If the event that caused the extinction of the dinosaurs 65 million years ago, at the end of the Cretaceous period, was a meteor strike followed by an extended dark 'winter', as many scientists believe, these habits would then have stood the mammals in good stead.

Biding their time

While dinosaurs grew in size and variety during their 165-million-year existence, early mammals stayed small and different species looked fairly similar to one another. Most were no bigger than modern-day shrews and few grew much larger than a rat, even though they had evolved from a group of cat and dog-sized therapsids (see page 57), called cynodonts. Indeed, the first mammals seem rather like an evolutionary experiment in miniaturisation. If they were, it worked. Whereas the cynodonts died out around 190 million years ago, probably as a result of competition with the dinosaurs, the mammals survived.

Although mammals remained small, evolution didn't stand still for them during the age of the dinosaurs. A number of different groups evolved, most of which subsequently disappeared, among them one that contained the opossum-sized

BABY OPOSSUM The southern opossum lives in Mexico and South America and, like kangaroos, is a member of the marsupial group of mammals. The young are born live but tiny (10 mm long) and make their way to a pouch where they stay for 60 days.

THE EARLY BIRDS

RECENT DISCOVERIES HAVE SHED LIGHT ON ONE OF THE MYSTERIES OF EVOLUTION – THE ANCESTRY OF BIRDS. It has long been known that birds existed alongside dinosaurs, but their ancestry was a puzzle. They appear suddenly in the fossil record, complete with wings and feathers, around 146 million years ago at the end of the Jurassic period. It is now thought likely that they actually evolved from dinosaurs.

Scientists already knew that the early birds shared certain characteristics with some dinosaurs. The first known bird was *Archaeopteryx*, and one small dinosaur, *Compsognathus*, had a very similar skeleton. But other fossil creatures from different groups also displayed avian characteristics and were equally likely candidates to be birds' closest relatives. The resemblance between *Compsognathus* and *Archaeopteryx* could have been an accident of evolution – scientists could not prove that the groups were linked.

Feathered dinosaurs

All that changed with the discovery of *Sinosauropteryx* in 1996. *Sinosauropteryx* was a small theropod (meat-eating) dinosaur, like *Compsognathus*. Its skeleton closely resembled those of both *Compsognathus* and *Archaeopteryx*. But whereas the only fossils anyone had found of *Compsognathus* were bones, *Sinosauropteryx* was exquisitely preserved. The outline of its skin could be seen, and emerging from it was a fluffy down of simple feathers.

Sinosauropteryx lived after *Archaeopteryx*, so it could not have been its ancestor, but the similarities in their skeletal structure and the presence of feathers were impossible to ignore. Clearly, these creatures were closely related, even though *Sinosauropteryx* represented a line of feathered dinosaurs that had stayed on the

DINOSAUR FEET? The scaled legs and clawed toes of a cassowary from New Guinea are reminiscent of the three-toed feet of meat-eating dinosaurs, from which birds are almost certainly descended.

ANCESTRAL THROW-BACK The chick of the hoatzin bird, from the rainforests of South America, has claws on its wings, which help it to clamber through the branches. Archaeopteryx *and other early birds had similar claws.*

ground. No one had found their common ancestor, but there was circumstantial evidence that such a creature must have existed. The case for birds having evolved from dinosaurs was all but made.

Since 1996, 14 more feathered dinosaurs have been found, all meat-eaters. None predates *Archaeopteryx*, but each find has added weight to the idea that birds descended from the theropod group. Some of these dinosaurs were covered with down, while others had more complex feathers, like those of *Archaeopteryx*.

One thing birds no longer have is teeth. They retained them until the latter part of the Cretaceous period – *Archaeopteryx* had teeth and so did many later species – but by the time of the mass extinction that ended the Cretaceous period (see page 59), the teeth were gone. They were lost in the evolutionary development of birds to save weight and make flight less of an effort.

At the same time, there must have been something else that was special about birds – perhaps their ability to fly or their smaller size. Whatever it was, that certain something enabled them to live on when the other dinosaurs died out.

T REX

ONE OF THE LARGEST LAND PREDATORS THAT HAS EVER EXISTED WAS THE MONSTROUS MEAT-EATING DINOSAUR, *TYRANNOSAURUS REX*, WHICH LIVED AT THE CLOSE OF THE DINOSAUR ERA. Popularly known simply as

T. rex, it had a huge head, which contained incredibly powerful jaw muscles, banana-sized serrated like steak knives and a mouth large enough to swallow an adult human whole. It attacked like a shark, charging in with its mouth wide open to tear a chunk from its prey before retreating to avoid the risk of injury. Once its prey was weak from blood loss, it went back in for the kill. It tore huge chunks of flesh and bone from its victim and bolted them down without chewing.

Tyrannosaurus rex probably had a powerful sense of smell to enable it to detect and track down food. According to CAT scans of a fossilised *T. rex* skull, its brain would have had huge olfactory bulbs (odour receptors), as do many modern creatures with an acute sense of smell. *Tyrannosaurus rex* was a solitary hunter and a top predator, but it would also have scavenged on dead carcasses if the opportunity presented itself. It may have been feathered. Not everybody likes this idea, but the objections are more aesthetic than scientific – a fluffy *T. rex* doesn't seem as frightening as a scaly one.

T. rex was first discovered in 1902 in fossil beds in what is now Montana in the USA, and it remained the largest known meat-eating dinosaur until 1993, when it lost that particular claim to *Giganotosaurus*, which lived earlier in what is now Argentina. Although *Giganotosaurus* was slightly longer than *T. rex*, its head was less heavily built and its teeth were smaller.

VITAL STATISTICS

SUPERORDER: Dinosauria
SUBORDER: Theropoda
TIME: 67–65 million years ago
DIET: Meat
DISTRIBUTION: What is now the USA and Canada
MAXIMUM LENGTH: 13 m
MAXIMUM WEIGHT: 5 tonnes

THE TURN OF THE
MAMMALS

FOR SEVERAL MILLION YEARS AFTER THE DINOSAURS HAD GONE, MAMMALS STAYED SMALL. The seasonal world of the Cretaceous period had changed to a more uniform, tropical one. The leaves of tropical plants are often guarded by toxins, making them hard to digest, even inedible, so few plant-eating mammals evolved and certainly no big ones. New carnivorous mammals remained rather small, too, since they only needed to be big enough to catch and kill insect-eating prey.

Nevertheless, several new mammal groups did appear, among them the earliest ancestors of the primates (humans, apes, monkeys), primitive rodents and the first bats. Others included a now extinct hoofed group called the condylarths. One of the most common of these seems to

VEGETARIAN VARIETY The Earth today supports a wide range of herbivorous mammals that exploit different plant niches, such as eating plants at different heights. Tough tropical greenery 65 million years ago, however, meant that plant-eaters were few at that time.

have been the rat-sized *Oxyclaenus*, which probably hunted early primates, such as the mouse-sized *Purgatorius*. Another rat-sized condylarth, *Protungulatum*, was the first plant-eating mammal, although plants formed only part of its diet.

Eventually, truly herbivorous condylarths evolved, and so did larger meat-eaters, which hunted them, including the cat-sized *Oxyaena* and hyena-like *Palaeonictis*. These predators were creodonts, a group with many of the features of modern carnivorous mammals, including shearing teeth for cutting through flesh. The largest meat-eaters of the period, however, were birds, such as the flightless *Gastornis*, which grew to 2 m tall and was armed with clawed feet and hooked bills. The last of their line died out in South America just 15 000 years ago.

ALL IN THE TEETH Modern meat-eating mammals such as lions share features with the early creodonts, including the pairs of shearing molars set back in the jaw.

A NEW DAWN

AROUND 55 MILLION YEARS AGO, THE EARTH EXPERIENCED A PERIOD OF GLOBAL WARMING CALLED THE THERMAL MAXIMUM. In just a few thousand years, the temperature of the planet increased by 6°C. With this came an explosion in mammal variety, which lasted for the next 23 million years.

At this point, the Earth was warmer and more humid than it had ever been. Not only were there no icecaps, there was rainforest at the poles. It was in this lush, green world that the ancestors of today's hoofed mammals first appeared. They had evolved from the condylarths, a group that was soon to go into decline and die out. Early species were fairly small, as many of their rainforest counterparts are today. They included the mouse-deer-sized *Diacodexis* and the first horse, *Hyracotherium* (formerly known as *Eohippus*), which was about the size of a small dog or a cat.

Over time, the climate cooled a little and the rainforest shrank. Towards the poles, it was replaced by drier, more open forest, which suited the evolution of larger mammals. Other new hoofed groups appeared, including the earliest rhinoceroses and tapirs, as well as now extinct groups, such as the brontotheres. Related to the rhinoceroses, tapirs and horses, the brontotheres started off similar in size and appearance to the first horse, *Hyracotherium*. Later types, however, such as *Brontotherium*, grew to 2.5 m at the shoulder and had growths on their heads like those of modern rhinoceroses – but made of bone instead of the tough matted hair of rhino horns. The largest land mammal ever, *Indricotherium*, was more closely related to rhinos than brontotheres. It reached over 5 m at the shoulder, 2 m more than a bull African elephant.

Monster meat-eaters to whales

Besides plant-eaters, new carnivorous hoofed mammals evolved. The most spectacular of these was *Andrewsarchus*, a colossal meat-eater that roamed what is now Mongolia around 40 million years ago. The largest meat-eating land mammal ever, *Andrewsarchus* stood 1.8 m high, was 5 m long and probably weighed around twice as much as a modern polar bear, perhaps 1500 kg. Its skull alone was more than 80 cm long.

The group of hoofed mammals to which *Andrewsarchus* belonged died out, but descendants of some of its earlier members took to the seas and live on as the dolphins and whales. The earliest known whale, *Basilosaurus*, appeared around 50 million years ago and was a huge predator, measuring around 18 m in length. Like the many large mammals that were simultaneously evolving on land, it found itself almost without competition – the giant marine reptiles, such as the pliosaurs and ichthyosaurs, which had populated the seas in the time of the dinosaurs, had similarly disappeared about 65 million years ago. The early whales

GROUND BREAKER *Verreaux's sifaka – a type of lemur from Madagascar – belongs to a group of primates called the prosimians, which began to appear around 55 million years ago. The ancestors of monkeys, apes and humans were also members of this group.*

BACK TO THE BLUE Dolphins and whales descended from a group of hoofed land predators that looked like wolves. Shore-living hunters, they began to spend more and more time in the water, until they evolved into fully marine animals around 50 million years ago.

were soon joined by the sea cows. Today, these herbivorous creatures are represented by the rare dugong and manatees, but they were once much more common and diverse.

Sea bears and early primates

Seals and sea lions did not appear until around 25 million years ago, having evolved from early bears, which belonged to the Carnivora – the group that contains all modern meat-eating mammals. The earliest members of the Carnivora appeared at about the same time as the first creodonts, but as the creodonts developed into more varied and ever larger forms, the carnivores remained small, their evolution held in check by creodont dominance.

Eventually, new types of carnivore appeared with subtly different features that enabled them to get the upper hand. Their backbones were slightly more flexible and their legs tended to be longer, and over millions of years they became direct competitors to the creodonts, slowly overtaking them as the chief predators on land. By the time some of these carnivores began to take to the sea, the creodonts were in decline, and around 8 million years ago, the last of them vanished.

At this stage, nearly all of the mammal groups we know today had appeared, including our own group, the primates, which had moved on a long way from the squirrel-like, insect-eating ancestral forms, such as *Purgatorius*. Now, the trees were filled with an array of different monkeys and members of our own family, the great apes. The next step, as far as humans are concerned, was the one that took some of these apes out of the trees and down to the ground.

UPRIGHT APE

Genetic studies show that our closest living relatives are the chimpanzees: more than 96 per cent of our DNA is identical to theirs.

ONCE, HUMANS WERE JUST ANOTHER KIND OF APE; NOW WE ARE THE CONTROLLING LIFE FORM ON EARTH. Our 'rise' has been remarkably rapid. Genetic studies show that our closest living relatives are the chimpanzees: more than 96 per cent of our DNA is identical to theirs. Chimpanzees and our own forebears branched off in different directions from a common ancestor around 8 million years ago. Chimpanzees changed little, remaining suited primarily for life in the trees. The apes that eventually became humans started to alter, their hind limbs gradually becoming better adapted for walking upright.

Why did this happen? According to many scientists, our ancestors were still living in trees in Africa when they began to adapt to walking on two feet. They probably hung from their arms and swung through the branches hand over hand, as orang-utans and gibbons do today. Also in common with these apes, they would have descended to the ground to cover the gaps between trees, walking on their hind legs with their arms held above them. Chimpanzees have also been observed walking in this way.

As the climate dried and forests thinned, the gaps between trees got wider and the need to make such crossings became more frequent. Individuals that could move more efficiently over the ground would have had an advantage over less able walkers.

HOLD ON TIGHT The thumb was a key development in primate evolution, enabling chimpanzees (left) to get a firm grip on tree branches. Farther along the evolutionary line, hominids and eventually humans, freed of the need to use their hands for walking and endowed with bigger brains, developed sophisticated manual skills using their thumbed hands. These included tool-making (above).

WALKING OUT OF THE PAST In 1976, scientists discovered a 25 m stretch of fossilised footprints near Laetoli in Tanzania, East Africa. They were around 3.5 million years old and similar to human prints but smaller, perhaps made by Australopithecus.

They would have survived and passed their genes, with this ability, to the next generation. Nevertheless, the earliest human ancestors were still essentially tree-dwellers. *Australopithecus afarensis*, the first truly two-legged member of the human ancestral line (the hominids), appeared only 3.9–3.5 million years ago.

From ape to human

Hominids may have moved permanently to the ground because their habitat was vanishing or because their mobility made it easier for them to find food there. By around 3 million years ago, Africa's animals were having to adapt to new changes in Earth's climate: as temperatures dropped, the continent dried out and rainforests retreated to be replaced by savannah and semi-arid lands. Amidst these changes, several new hominid species evolved. Some, such as *Paranthropus boisei*, became entirely herbivorous, living on tubers and grass; others – *Homo habilis*, for example – turned to eating meat.

Since meat was rich in calories and easy to digest, *Homo habilis* had energy to spare. Increased brain size and more brainpower permitted the creation of simple tools, and even larger-brained hominids followed. Their hands, meanwhile, had evolved from powerful swinging hooks into delicate instruments capable of complex movement and subtle manipulation. From scavengers and grabbers of small creatures, our ancestors turned into intelligent hunters.

The precise path that led from early hominids to our own species, *Homo sapiens*, is a subject of debate. What is certain is that we are the only surviving hominids. Some, such as *Homo habilis*, died out long before we appeared, but others shared the Earth with us. The last to go – perhaps wiped out by us – were the neanderthals (*Homo neanderthalensis*), who existed in Europe until just 24 000 years ago.

IN 1974, SCIENTISTS FOUND A TINY SKELETON IN ETHIOPIA.
The fossilised remains turned out to be those of an adult female around 3.2 million years old. Nicknamed Lucy, she was classified as *Australopithecus afarensis*, the first of her kind to be discovered. In life she would have been about 1 m tall and 27 kg in weight.

HOMO ERECTUS, a hominid that went extinct 400 000 years ago, is credited with harnessing fire, perhaps 500 000 years ago.

THE EARLIEST KNOWN FOSSILS OF *HOMO SAPIENS* (our species) date from 195 000 years ago.

TIMELINE OF LIFE

IF THE EARTH'S HISTORY was condensed into a single year, life would appear in the first week of March, and all life would remain single-celled until the end of October. The bulk of the timeline below shows the history of life after that point, starting with the Cambrian period, when the seas filled with a carnival of new creatures. Later, during the Devonian period – the equivalent of early December – the first air-breathing fish pulled themselves onto the land. At the end of the Permian period, on what would be December 12, life was put to the test when a mass extinction swept the planet, wiping out more than 95 per cent of all the life forms in the oceans and perhaps 99 per cent of all vertebrate species on land. Some species survived, however, and life flourished once more from the Triassic period to the present.

CAMBRIAN SEABED DWELLERS

Some of the most common fossils in rocks from the Cambrian period and after are of trilobites. They were arthropods – members of the animal phylum that includes insects, arachnids and crustaceans – which lived on the seabed. They existed from the Cambrian until the mass extinction at the end of the Permian.

PRECAMBRIAN PROKARYOTES

For just under half of the time that life has existed on Earth, the only living things were cyanobacteria and other prokaryotes, single-celled organisms without cell nuclei. Traces of these ancient organisms survive in the oldest known fossils (above). Dating back more than 3.5 billion years, they are of stromatolites, mats of cyanobacteria mixed with sediment. Even today, in terms of numbers, prokaryotes vastly

PRECAMBRIAN ALGAE

Eosphaera was one of the earliest organisms with a cell nucleus (eukaryotes). It was a single-celled algae which lived in the seas and generated its own food using sunlight to power photosynthesis. *Eosphaera* appeared around 2 billion years ago. Single-celled algae very like it still exist in the oceans today.

4.6 BILLION TO 550 MILLION YEARS AGO
PRECAMBRIAN

PRECAMBRIAN

CAMBRIAN
550-505 MILLION
YEARS AGO (MYA)

ORDOVICIAN
505-438 MYA

SILURIAN
438-408 MYA

DEVONIAN
408-360 MYA

CARBONIFEROUS
360-286 MYA

PERMIAN
286-245 MYA

PALAEOZOIC

550 TO 245 MYA
PALAEOZOIC

JURASSIC BIRDS

Archaeopteryx is the oldest known bird, from the end of the Jurassic period, about 144 million years ago. Recent discoveries suggest that birds evolved directly from meat-eating dinosaurs. During the Cretaceous period, almost all birds had teeth.

TRIASSIC ARRIVALS

Coelophysis was one of the first dinosaurs. Like most other early dinosaurs – which appeared around the same time as mammals, 230 million years ago – *Coelophysis* was a meat-eater. Dinosaurs differed from their predecessors in having a more upright stance, with their legs tucked beneath their bodies rather than sprawled out to the sides.

PLIOCENE PREDATOR

Smilodon was one of the largest of the sabre-toothed cats. Although about 30 cm shorter than a modern lion, it was nearly twice as heavy. *Smilodon* is thought to have hunted in groups, as lions do today. It existed from the Pliocene epoch to the end of the Pleistocene epoch, just 10000 years ago.

PALAEOCENE
65-57 MYA

EOCENE
57-34 MYA

65 TO 1.8 MYA
CENOZOIC
TERTIARY PERIOD

OLIGOCENE
34-23 MYA

MIOCENE
23-5 MYA

TERTIARY

CRETACEOUS
144-65 MYA

MESOZOIC

245 TO 65 MYA
MESOZOIC

JURASSIC
208-144 MYA

TRIASSIC
245-208 MYA

PLEISTOCENE
1.8 MILLION TO
10 000 YEARS AGO

1.8 MYA TO PRESENT
CENOZOIC
QUATERNARY PERIOD

PLIOCENE 5-1.8 MYA

HOLOCENE
10 000 YEARS AGO
TO PRESENT

QUATERNARY

CYCLES OF
CHANGE

3

CLIMATE CHANGE IS SO OFTEN IN THE NEWS, WE TEND TO THINK OF IT AS A RECENT PHENOMENON. While there is little doubt that the current rate of change is greater than at most times in the past, the fact is that the Earth's climate has gone through periods of change ever since life began. And every one of those periods of change affected the distribution of species around the world. Many factors combine to create alterations in climate. Most are manifestations of natural cycles of change, some of which take place over millennia or eons, some over decades and some over a single year. Ice ages, which affect the climate on Earth and shape its landscape, result from cycles that take place over thousands of years. This glacial valley on New Zealand's South Island was carved by a vast sheet of ice during the last ice age, which ended around 10 000 years ago.

71º 1' NORTH

NORTH AND SOUTH The Neumayer Channel in Antarctica (right) and Nordkapp (North Cape) in Norway (above) lie on similar latitudes, but temperatures at Neumayer are much lower than those at Nordkapp. This is because Antarctica is a continental landmass permanently covered in ice, whereas the Arctic Ocean stores heat, preventing temperatures on the surrounding landmasses falling too low.

NORDKAPP — 70º N

Tropic of Cancer

EQUATOR

Tropic of Capricorn

NEUMAYER CHANNEL — 70º S

THE CHANGING FACE OF EARTH

ARCTIC LANDSCAPE Nordkapp is situated on the island of Magerøya in the extreme north of Norway. During the short, cool Arctic summer, the ground unfreezes enough for lichens, mosses and arctic flowers to appear.

THE MAP OF THE EARTH WE KNOW TODAY IS A SNAPSHOT OF THE PLANET'S EVER-CHANGING FACE. Since the continents first formed, they have moved slowly but surely around the surface of the planet. And as they have moved and rearranged themselves across the face of the planet they have brought change – to the climate, to the landscape and to life itself. The process driving all this movement is called plate tectonics and it is made possible by the Earth's layered structure.

The Earth has three main layers. At the centre is the hot core, surrounded by a layer of molten rock, or magma, called the mantle. The rocky outer skin is the crust. Far from being a solid shell, the crust is made up of sections, or plates, of varying shapes and sizes that fit together like jigsaw pieces and form the foundations of continents and ocean basins. They float on the semi-liquid rock of the outer mantle. Convection currents in the mantle keep the plates constantly on the move. The plates are tightly packed together, and as they move some are forced beneath others at their edges. Elsewhere, plates are pulled apart and magma rises up to fill the gaps, forming new crust.

Earthquakes and volcanoes are sudden and dramatic manifestations of plate tectonics – the only ones we have a chance of witnessing during our short lives on the planet. Over a much longer time frame, the effects of plate movement are far-reaching. Whole continents shift, changing position in relation to other continents, to the oceans and to the Equator and poles. When plates diverge, ecosystems split as they are dragged apart; where plates collide, the crust along their edges buckles up to form mountain ranges. These factors have produced profound fluctuations and changes in the planet's climate and in the development and distribution of life.

Polar opposites

The arrangement of landmasses, particularly in relation to the North and South Poles, has a profound effect on the planet's climate. As the continents move, they can trigger change in the global climate, with far-reaching effects for life.

Discounting altitude, temperatures drop as one travels north or south from the Equator, but it becomes colder quicker

> ### ROCKS OF THE EARTH'S CRUST
> The plates that make up the Earth's crust are formed from solid rock. Geologists classify rocks into three main types:
> **IGNEOUS** These are formed by volcanic eruptions or the cooling of magma beneath the Earth's surface. Granite is the most common igneous rock.
> **SEDIMENTARY** Particles eroded from rocks form sediment, which is buried and compressed into layers of new rock. Common sedimentary rocks include limestone, sandstone and shale. Around three-quarters of all the world's land surface is covered by sedimentary rocks. Changes in the rock layers record changes in climate and vegetation.
> **METAMORPHIC** These rocks are formed when existing igneous or sedimentary rocks are altered by extreme heat and pressure deep below the Earth's surface. Common metamorphic rocks include slate and marble.

as one heads south. Temperatures are lower at the edge of the Antarctic Circle than at the same latitude in the north. This is because the North Pole is covered by ocean. Although the ocean is covered by a floating icecap, the water beneath never drops far below 0°C. (Near the surface it can get down to -1.8°C, the freezing point of seawater.) In effect, the Arctic Ocean – which is linked to other oceans by currents – acts as a heat reservoir.

ANTARCTIC ICE Even in summer, snow-covered peaks soar above the 25 km long Neumayer Channel and glaciers pour into the water and shatter. This ice-covered landmass was once in the Northern Hemisphere and supported life.

64° 47′ SOUTH

MARSUPIAL MAJORITY

The splitting off of continents and smaller blocks of land has led to some groups of animals becoming isolated, allowing them to evolve along different lines from creatures elsewhere on Earth. Australia is famous for being a land dominated by marsupials, with around three-quarters of the Earth's 266 marsupial species living there. When Australia broke away from the other southern continents there were no placental mammals aboard, so the marsupials were free to evolve into a huge range of forms without competition, occupying niches that are occupied by placental mammals in other parts of the world. The koala bear (below) lives in the trees of eastern Australia, where it exists almost entirely on a diet of eucalyptus leaves.

In contrast, the South Pole is covered by the vast continent of Antarctica. Without the warmth of the ocean to moderate its temperature, it is far colder than the Arctic: temperatures as low as -88°C have been recorded. The icecap over Antarctica is much larger than the one at the Arctic. Sitting on land, it covers an area of 13.9 million km^2 and is 2 km thick – hiding all but the tallest mountain peaks.

The presence or absence of land around the poles has affected changes in the planet's climate. When landmasses are concentrated near the poles, snow and ice can accumulate and glaciation can take place because the ice can keep on spreading until it reaches warmer latitudes, whereas the spread of ice over the sea is limited by the warmth and salinity of seawater. The presence of land around the poles also has a great impact on sea levels: when water is locked up in the icecaps there is less of it in the oceans and more of the Earth's crust is exposed as land. Antarctica's icecap contains around 70 per cent of the world's fresh water, and if it melted ocean levels would rise considerably.

Mountains

Mountain ranges mark the zones where converging plates meet. Generally, the higher the range the more recently it formed. The world's highest mountains, the Himalayas, began rising when the Indian subcontinental plate crashed into Asia between 40 and 50 million years ago. Ancient rock on the sea floor between them was gradually pushed upwards to form the mountains. The plates are still moving and the mountains continue to rise. Older ranges, such as the Rockies in North America, which formed around 70 million years ago, were once as high but have since been worn down by weathering and erosion.

Mountain ranges can significantly affect the climate of neighbouring regions, and this has a powerful influence on the direction evolution takes. Mountains act as barriers to rain, and in many parts of the world they form clear dividing lines between wet and dry areas. The Andes run down the western side of South America with the Amazon rain forest to their east and the Atacama Desert, the continent's largest desert, to their west. The prevailing winds blow from east to west, and when they meet the mountains air is forced upwards. As the air rises it cools and the moisture in it begins to condense, forming clouds. The moisture then falls as rain, which collects and flows back eastwards into the vast rain forest basin. By the time the air has risen high enough to pass over the peaks it is bone dry, so virtually no rain falls on the western slopes of the mountains, making the Atacama the driest place on Earth. The region is so arid that even mountains reaching as high as 6885 m are completely free of glaciers.

In many ways, Australia is South America's geographical opposite. Its prevailing winds also blow from east to west, but it has a mountainous spine, the Great Dividing Range, running down its east rather than its west side. As a result, Australia has only a thin band of lush, green, forested terrain down its east coast, while the rain shadow to the west of the mountains stretches all the way to Perth and the North West Cape.

Mountains block rain, but even where they are absent land becomes drier the farther it is from the sea. The deserts and arid lands of Mongolia and other parts of central Asia are starved of rain simply because they lie so far from the coast. In certain periods in the Earth's past, such as in the early Mesozoic era (250 million years ago), the continents have been bunched together. During these periods vast areas of land lay a great distance from the sea. Conditions then favoured plants and animals that could cope with little water, such as seed-bearing plants and reptiles. At other times, such as during the Jurassic period (205-135 million years ago), the continents were more fragmented and a greater proportion of land was closer to the sea. This created a wetter climate that sustained dense forest over much larger areas of land.

DIVIDING LINE *The Himalayas, seen here from space, are one of the youngest mountain ranges. To their north is the cold, arid Tibetan plateau; to their south, the fertile Ganges plain. Volcanoes are visible proof of the tectonic forces changing the Earth's face. Piton de la Fournaise on Réunion (inset) is one of the most active volcanoes on Earth. It has erupted over 150 times since 1640.*

BLOWING HOT AND COLD

GLOBAL WARMING IS NOTHING NEW. Over the past 2 million years there have been times when the climate was far hotter, with sea levels much higher than now, interspersed with very cold spells. These past climate fluctuations have played a big part in the way species are presently distributed across the Earth. All species have an optimum temperature and humidity range in which they can live, so their distribution is affected by their climatic requirements. If species members are living at the extremes of this range, they are vulnerable to competition from other species. When the climate changes, a species may not be able to compete with better-adapted ones; some move, while others die out.

Although global temperatures are currently rising, the world today is not particularly warm compared to some earlier eras in Earth's history. What is new is the impact of human activity on the Earth's climate, and the speed at which change is happening. Global warming as we now know it is the result of increasing levels of greenhouse gases, such as carbon dioxide, in the atmosphere. These act like the glass in a greenhouse, trapping the Sun's heat and preventing it bouncing back out into space, as it otherwise would. High levels of greenhouse gases in the atmosphere have caused or magnified previous warm spells on Earth, but they are not the only factors that have brought about changes in the Earth's climate.

The Earth's albedo

The planet's albedo (from the Latin *albus*, for white) is its reflectiveness, and this is an important factor contributing to temperature. Basically, a surface that reflects most of the light that hits it looks bright and has a high albedo, whereas one that absorbs most of the light looks dull and has a low albedo. Land reflects far more light and heat back into space than water does. Ice is even more reflective. Therefore, the distribution of land and the size of the polar icecaps have a huge influence on the planet's overall average temperature.

At the start of the Jurassic period, most of the land on Earth was gathered into one single supercontinent called

ANCESTRAL OUTFIT A female grey seal watches over her pup on a beach in Norfolk, in England. All grey seal pups enter the world with white coats. These are an evolutionary leftover from the last ice age, when the shores on which they were born were covered with ice and snow.

Pangaea. This had two halves joined by a 'neck' at the Equator. The vast majority of land lay in what are now the subtropical and temperate regions. There was no land over the poles, and the icecaps were virtually non-existent. This arrangement gave the Earth an extremely low albedo. Far more of the Sun's energy was soaked up and retained than it is today: temperatures were estimated to be about 10°C higher on average than today. Plant growth increased, driving the evolution of ever larger plant-eating dinosaurs. In the warming oceans, algae bloomed.

As photosynthesising organisms grew in number, the amount of oxygen in the atmosphere increased. At its peak oxygen comprised about 30 per cent of the air, in contrast to the 21 per cent it makes up today. Carbon dioxide levels also increased, reaching five times their current level. This was partly due to the increased biomass of animal life on Earth. The productivity of the Earth during the Jurassic period was a direct result of its low albedo and warmer land and seas. The higher levels of carbon dioxide added to that warmth and accelerated plant growth. Plants would have been able to support much

ICE-AGE ERAS

Hundreds of ice ages have come and gone in the Earth's past. They were not randomly scattered – they occurred in four distinct blocks.

ICE AGE	TIMESPAN	COMMENTS
Late Proterozoic	800–600 million years ago (mya)	With most organisms still confined to the seas, the impact on life was minimal
Ordovician and Silurian	460–430 mya	These ice ages were less severe than those before or after them
Pennsylvanian and Permian	350–250 mya	As in all ice ages, conditions remained moderate to warm in the tropics
Neogene to Quaternary	4 mya to the present day	There have been more than 60 individual ice ages in the past 2 million years alone

heavier browsing by larger plant-eating animals as they would have repaired themselves much more quickly by growing new leaves than they can today.

Causes of ice ages

The continents are continuously on the move, but the pace at which they travel is slow and they take tens of millions of years to move far enough to change the Earth's climate significantly. Other processes occur much faster. Studies of the Earth's sedimentary rocks have revealed evidence for cycles of glaciation – recurring ice ages with warmer periods in between. Although this evidence can be obtained only for the last 700 000 years, scientists assume that the cyclical pattern shown in the rocks goes back much farther.

Ice ages have come and gone at intervals of about 19 000, 24 000, 43 000 and 97 000 years, periods that coincide closely with alterations in the Earth's tilt and orbital path around the Sun. The Earth's tilt is thought to shift every 41 000 years from 22° to 24.5°, before moving back again. When the axis tilts at 22°, the poles receive a lower than usual amount of sunlight through the year, allowing icecaps to build up and expand. As the angle increases towards 24.5°, the poles receive more sunlight in summer, causing an increased seasonal melt. The amount of permanent ice on the planet drops, and so does the Earth's albedo, causing a rise in sea levels and global temperatures.

The 97 000-year period matches a different cycle: the time it takes for the shape of the Earth's orbit to change. The Earth's path around the Sun varies from almost circular to slightly elliptical. When the orbit is elliptical, the Earth experiences warmer summers and colder winters. These conditions correspond to interglacial periods. When the Earth's orbit is close to circular, the summers are at their coolest. Less winter snowfall melts, and when more falls the following winter it is compacted to ice, which slowly builds up.

The third cause of ice ages – and the one probably responsible for the 19 000- and 24 000-year cycles – is a slight wobble in the Earth's spin. This occurs because the Earth is not spherical, but has a slight bulge at the Equator. This affects the timing of the equinoxes (the times of year when the Earth is farthest from the Sun), which impacts on the planet's seasonality.

The impact of ice

The advance and retreat of the icecaps is directly responsible for much of the planet's modern landscape. The bowl-shaped valleys common in the world's colder temperate zones were carved out

by glaciers during the last ice age, which ended just 10 000 years ago (Earth is currently near the peak of an interglacial period). The world's coastlines have also altered greatly and they will change again. As recently as 8000 years ago Britain was linked to Europe by a land bridge, which disappeared as the icecaps retreated and sea levels rose. Although ice ages change the landscape, they have an even greater impact on the evolution of life. The colder conditions force animals and plants either to adapt or to move towards the Equator ahead of the advancing ice. At the same time, movement between continents is easier as sea levels are lower and land bridges open up, allowing species to migrate and colonise new areas.

One creature that evolved during the last ice age was the woolly mammoth. Like many ice-age mammals, it had a long, shaggy coat to keep out the cold and other adaptations to survive in the snow-covered tundra. The mammoth was unsuited to a warmer climate and died out as the ice retreated, although its extinction was hastened by man, who hunted it.

As the planet comes out of an ice age, species that are adapted to the cold follow the receding ice back towards the poles, but some may find their passage blocked by seas that appear, or reappear, as ocean levels rise again.

WOODLAND VARIATION Spring carpets of bluebells are unique to Britain. During the last ice age, as the icecap spread south, woodlands and woodland flowers were pushed southwards, but bluebells survived because their new shoots begin growing underground, even under snow and ice. When the icecap retreated, bluebells had little competition as they recolonised areas. Although other plants gradually spread northwards, the flooding of the English Channel blocked this migration. In North America, there were no barriers to prevent the northward spread of plants as the ice retreated, and woodlands now support a much greater variety of flora in spring (inset).

CHANGES OVER DECADES

VARIABILITY IS BUILT INTO THE GLOBAL CLIMATE SYSTEM THROUGH NATURAL CYCLES OF ATMOSPHERIC DISTURANCE. These cycles operate over years rather than millennia, and can have an impact on weather patterns around the world. One of the best-known and most significant is the El Niño phenomenon. El Niño is a natural, irregular cycle of change in the Pacific Ocean that occurs once every five or so years, initiated by changes in atmospheric pressure on either side of the Pacific. During an El Niño, warm surface water builds up along the western shores of South America, blocking the cold, nutrient-rich, up-welling currents that normally bathe this coast. At the same time, the usually warm surface waters of the western Pacific off Indonesia and Australia cool. This has the effect of switching the climate in both areas. The arid western coast of South America experiences violent storms, while the tropical rains of Indonesia and north-eastern Australia dry up.

Although the El Niño phenomenon has only been properly understood for a few decades, the cycle itself is ancient. Many plants and animals that are directly affected by it have evolved mechanisms to cope. Some have even adapted to take advantage of the changes it brings. In

COLD COMFORT Galápagos penguins are the most northerly of all penguins. They were brought to the Galápagos Islands by the Humboldt Current, which brings cold waters and nutrients north from Antarctica. During El Niño years the penguin population declines. With the cold waters cut off, fish stocks dwindle and adults find it hard to catch enoug to feed themselves, let alone hungry young.

Australia, El Niño causes drought and fire, and many species of eucalyptus, which dominate the forests there, have evolved to withstand the flames. Some re-sprout from their trunks and branches soon after fire has passed. Others grow anew from seeds released from resinous pods by the heat of the flames.

El Niño can have an impact on the weather as far away as Europe, as does La Niña – El Niño's less well-known but equally powerful counterpart. La Niñas are caused by the sudden cooling of surface waters in the central and eastern Pacific. They often follow extreme El Niños and have the opposite impact on climate, causing normally humid or wet areas to experience even more severe storms than they are used to.

Other cycles of change include the Pacific Decadal Oscillation, which occurs in the North Pacific and affects the weather in western North America; and the North Atlantic Oscillation, which affects North America and Europe. The North Atlantic Oscillation has an irregular cycle lasting several decades. Its main impact is on atmospheric pressure over the Arctic. When that is low, as it was in 2007, Europe's winters are mild and wet. After the switch, which is due to happen in the near future, winters in this part of the world should become more extreme.

Solar cycles

Many scientists believe that variations in solar activity might also be responsible for changes in the Earth's climate. Solar activity is known to vary slightly over an 11-year cycle. Periods of high activity are marked by peaks in the number of sunspots – dark patches on the Sun's surface that last between an hour and one month and can be easily measured. Some studies appear to show a correlation between increased sunspot counts and slightly raised average surface temperatures on Earth.

The last major dip in the Earth's average temperature was the so-called Little Ice Age, which lasted from the 13th to the 19th centuries. The middle – and coldest – part coincided closely with the Maunder Minimum, a period of decreased solar activity when sunspots became increasingly rare.

OUT OF THE ASHES El Niño is a natural cycle and organisms that live in areas closely affected by it have evolved to cope. Eucalyptus trees in Australia have become fire tolerant and quickly sprout new growth after the blazes that El Niño years bring.

ANNUAL CHANGE

AWAY FROM THE EQUATOR, THE MOST EXTREME WEATHER CHANGES ARE ONES THAT WE LIVE WITH FROM YEAR TO YEAR. The cycle of the seasons sees vast swings in temperature and weather that take place in a matter of months. The only reason that we do not see these changes as cataclysmic is because – like many animals and plants – we have evolved and changed our behaviour to cope with them.

SPRING

SUMMER

The changing seasons result from Earth's axis being tilted. As the Earth circles the Sun, different regions receive different amounts of sunlight at different times of the year. During June, July and August, the North Pole (one tip of the axis) points slightly towards the Sun, while the South Pole (the other tip) is in permanent shadow. Northern countries have longer day lengths at this time and receive more direct sunlight than those at equivalent latitudes in the south. During December, January and February, that situation is reversed. The nearer to the poles, the longer the periods of summer light and winter darkness.

Seasonal changes require adaptations on the part of plants and animals. Many reproduce on a seasonal cycle, while other physical and behavioural adaptations in animals have developed to cope with the changes in temperature and in the

food supply. The greater the seasonal variations, the greater th adaptations needed to cope with the changes.

In physical terms our species has altered very little sinc it first appeared. Humans are better adapted naturally to cope with heat than cold. Our bodies have sweat glands (unlike thos of many other mammals), which enable us to take advantage o the cooling effect of evaporation. Prolonged exposure to strong sunlight causes our skin to produce the dark pigment melanin, which protects it from damaging ultraviolet rays. We have adapted our behaviour in order to cope with cold. Humans have learned to master fire and to make extra insulating layers in th form of clothes. Buildings help to keep us alive through winter colder parts of the world. The combination of large brains and dextrous hands has enabled humans to conquer seasonal change

LEAVES CHANGE COLOUR
IN AUTUMN AS THE PRODUCTION OF CHLOROPHYLL WITHIN THEM SLOWS DOWN.
As this green pigment disappears the other, underlying pigments, which range from yellow to brown, become visible.

THE SEASONAL CYCLE The yearly cycle of the seasons is reflected by changes in temperate broadleaf trees, such as this oak. In spring, lengthening daylight triggers the growth of new leaves, which photosynthesise using energy from the Sun to fuel the tree's growth. Lessening light levels in autumn trigger changes in leaf colour as photosynthesis diminishes. As autumn turns to winter, the trees jettison their leaves to save energy in the cold season.

CHANGING COLOUR
and leaf drop are due to decreasing day length. Trees near artificial sources of light keep their leaves longer than those growing elsewhere.

SEASONS ARE MOST EXTREME AT THE POLES.
Here winter is not only cold but completely dark for more than two months.

FACTS

AUTUMN

Other animals deal with winter in different ways. Some, such as birds, migrate, heading for warmer climes before the frosts arrive and food supplies start to run out. Others retreat into burrows or other sheltered spots to hibernate, slowing their metabolisms down to the bare minimum required to stay alive. All sorts of animals hibernate, from mammals such as bears to insects such as ladybirds. Although some hibernate alone, many gather together in large numbers to share their body heat.

Of course, not all animals hibernate or migrate. Some, such as squirrels, survive the winter by eating food that they have stored away earlier in the year. Others change their diets to cope with the disappearance of their normal food. Moose, for instance, turn to eating bark rather than leaves and shoots as autumn ends and winter begins.

WINTER

In temperate parts of the Northern Hemisphere, winter is defined by the fact that the majority of trees are deciduous and lose their leaves. This itself is an adaptation to the cold weather and shorter days that this season brings. Leaves are the factories that trees use to produce food, but they need water and sunlight in order to produce energy for growth. In winter, both of these are in short supply. For much of the time moisture is locked up in the ground as ice and any sunlight that does reach the branches is weaker than in summer, as well as lasting for fewer hours of the day. Leaves cost energy to maintain and it is more efficient for these plants to lose them and generate new ones in the spring. Coniferous trees have smaller leaves better able to survive the rigours of winter: they benefit from retaining their leaves as they can start photosynthesising earlier in the spring.

THE SHIMMER
TAPEST

ING
RY

4

LIFE ON EARTH NEVER STAYS THE SAME
FOR LONG: NEW SPECIES ARE CONSTANTLY
EVOLVING, WHILE ESTABLISHED ONES
BECOME EXTINCT. The world's flora and fauna
have been changing ever since they first
appeared and the process by which they do
this is called evolution. In essence, evolution
is the result of natural pressures acting on
the variety inherent within each species.
Individuals that are better able to cope with
those pressures, for whatever reason, are more
likely to reproduce. The traits that enabled
them to cope are then passed on to, and
amplified in, the next generation. The pressures
that drive evolution may come from the
environment, from other species or from within
the species itself. The evolution of the male
peacock's tail was driven by female mate
choice, just one source of natural pressure.

LIFE'S DRIVING FORCE

EVOLUTION IS THE GREATEST OF ALL FORCES OF CHANGE IN LIVING THINGS AND IS RESPONSIBLE FOR THE HUGE VARIETY OF LIFE ON THE PLANET. Every species of every life form that has ever existed came into being because of evolution. The process began as soon as the first living thing started to alter. Exactly what that life form looked like is a mystery, but in a way its appearance is irrelevant. What mattered, in terms of what happened next, was that it had the capacity to change. If life had not been able to adapt in response to the environment around it, it would have died out long ago.

All in the genes

The ability of animals to change with each generation is due to genetic variety within each species. Every individual inherits a set of genes from each parent, and these combine to create something entirely new. With the exception of identical twins, which form from the division of a single fertilised egg, no two offspring of the same parents are genetically exactly alike. Every sperm and every egg cell have a unique complement of genetic material, so each individual receives a slightly different combination of genes from its parents. This variety is built not just into animal species, but into all organisms that reproduce sexually, including the majority of plants and fungi. Bacteria and other organisms that reproduce asexually, by budding off, have far less in-built variety, but evolution occurs in them, too, through occasional genetic mutations.

WINTER COLOURS The willow ptarmigan of northern North America changes its plumage to match the seasons. In summer, it is mottled brown and white; in winter, its whole body is white so that it blends in with its snowy surroundings.

Evolution does not happen randomly. Genes and the physical attributes they influence are naturally selected if they increase an organism's chances of survival and the likelihood of it producing offspring of its own. The three main pressures that drive the process are: the need to find food while avoiding being eaten by a predator; the battle to breed; and the need to fit in with particular environmental conditions, responding and adapting to short- and long-term changes in the environment.

The results of evolution are all around us. The fact that there are animals on land is due to the evolution of lungs and other organs that enabled their ancestors to breathe air. Movement on land is facilitated by legs, which evolved from fins. Even the organs and tissues that enable our senses to operate evolved from more primitive structures in past creatures. The evolution of the eye, for instance, can be traced back through ancestral creatures to the simple light-sensitive patches of tissue on certain worms and other primitive invertebrates.

Evolution has also had an impact beyond living things: it has helped to shape the Earth. Without the evolution of photosynthesis, there would be no oxygen in the atmosphere. And without the evolution of plants, fungi and other land organisms, there would be no soil.

Work in progress

The theory of evolution through natural selection was first set out in the mid-19th century by Charles Darwin in his book *On the Origin of Species*, published in 1859. The first reaction of the public to it was one of shock. The suggestion that our own species was descended, however distantly, from more primitive apes, rather than created by God in his own image, was one that many people found difficult to come to terms with. Some people still cannot accept the idea, but in general, scientific reasoning prevailed and Darwin's theory of evolution through natural selection became widely accepted. Today, it is regarded as one of the most important contributions – perhaps the most important – that anyone has made to our understanding of life on Earth.

The implications of Darwin's theory were profound. Being the self-engrossed species that we are, we became obsessed with how evolution through natural selection affected us and what it said about our position in the scheme of things. Before long, the general perception of *Homo sapiens* had altered from our being a flawed manifestation of God to being the ultimate peak of evolutionary development. The reality is much less grand. We, like every other species on Earth, are a work in progress. Ten million years from now it is quite likely that our species will have changed a great deal – if we are still here.

Evolution, by its nature, does not stop. As long as the pressures driving it exist, it will continue to affect all life on Earth. Every species of living organism is subject to this driving force. Sometimes the resulting changes take thousands or even millions of years to occur, but in many cases they happen much faster.

SUPERSURVIVOR
Our own species has helped to drive evolution. Modern medicine has turned the human body into a hostile place for micro-organisms. Some have become extinct, while others have adapted and evolved. One of the great survivors is the bacterium *Staphylococcus aureus*, which can cause serious infection if it gets into the bloodstream. Most *Staphylococcus aureus* are killed by antibiotics, but one strain – methicillin-resistant *Staphylococcus aureus*, or MRSA – has evolved resistance, giving it a great evolutionary advantage.

HUNTER
VERSUS HUNTED

EVOLUTIONARY EQUALS The lion is an efficient hunter, but it has to be to prey on species such as the kudu that are fast and agile.

THE NEVER-ENDING BATTLE BETWEEN PREDATORS AND PREY IS ONE OF THE STRONGEST DRIVERS BEHIND EVOLUTIONARY CHANGE. The necessity to chase moving food has favoured species that could develop a fast turn of speed or a degree of group cooperation. Other predators have evolved colours and markings that help them to blend into the background as they wait for prey to come within striking range. The hunted often use variations on the same techniques to keep themselves from becoming someone's next meal. This never-ending battle has led to many developments in the animal kingdom, including that of speed. The quicker or more agile individuals escape – or catch their prey. Speed is most useful for those animals that live in the open, both on land and in the sea. For prey species with

FAST MOVER The pine marten has evolved sharp claws and a bushy tail that aid agility and balance as it chases prey through the branches. It is one of the few creatures with enough speed to catch a red squirrel.

time. If the prey animal can dodge the first attack, it usually escapes. Sprinting is exhausting and animals cannot maintain high speeds for long. Some predators rely on stamina and endurance instead; if they can maintain a steady speed they will eventually catch up as their victim tires. This method is used by slower pack hunters, such as hyenas and members of the dog family.

Working together

Many species have developed the ability to hunt in groups. This increases the individual's chances of catching prey, and enables predators to catch animals that are too large or too quick for them to tackle on their own. On land, group hunting is practised by a variety of carnivores, including lions and wolves. In the oceans, species such as dolphins, porpoises and humpback whales work in groups to catch prey. One feature that all these animals have in common is the ability to cooperate and coordinate their behaviour. This requires a significant degree of intelligence, and group hunting is a major force behind the evolution of more complex brains.

nowhere to hide and no obstacles to put between themselves and predators, speed is essential for staying alive. The ability to dodge and turn suddenly is important, too: making a predator miss and over-run can gain an animal a vital split second that might make the difference between life and death.

Predators, by the same token, must be able to match or exceed the speed of their prey. Some, such as the cheetah, rely on sprinting, accelerating rapidly to a speed greater than its prey can manage in order to catch up and knock it to the ground. For this to work, the predator usually has to get everything right first

PRICKLY CUSTOMERS

Unlike animals, plants cannot run away from their attackers. Some, like the fleshy saguaro cactus of the US south-west, have evolved spines as a defence against being eaten. As with all evolutionary processes, the appearance of spines was not predetermined but was naturally selected over time. Plants that were slightly more spiky than their counterparts were less palatable and so were likely to be left alone. They were the ones that survived to become parents of the next generation, and the genes that caused their spininess were passed on.

All sorts of animals form groups for safety, including many species of insects, fish and birds, so clearly the drive to evolve group behaviour is strong. Being part of a group helps an individual's chances of survival in many ways. For the hunted, groups can provide a means of defence. When threatened, large herbivores such as musk oxen and elephants group together to form a defensive wall around their young. All herd animals use the group as an early warning system, many pairs of eyes, ears and nostrils being more likely to detect a predator than one pair. And an individual is harder for a predator to pick out and target if it is part of a group, whether a herd, flock or shoal.

Becoming invisible

Of course, not all animals live in groups. Many spend most of their lives on their own, and have usually evolved other means of avoiding predators. One of the most common means is camouflage. This feature, too, evolved through natural selection.

DECEPTIVE APPEARANCE This stick insect is almost indistinguishable from the stalk of grass it is clinging to.

Individuals of a species that were born with a colour or pattern that most closely matched their background survived and went on to breed, while more obvious individuals were eaten. The same process selects for mimicry, where a species resembles an object, such as a twig or leaf, in its environment. Camouflage is also useful to predators. For them, the advantage is in being able to get close to prey without being seen. Predators with colours or patterns that enable them to do this are more likely to catch prey, so survive to pass on their livery to future generations.

Camouflage is common in the animal kingdom, and to get round it predators have evolved ever more acute senses. Birds, in particular, have extremely good vision. They react to movement as well as to subtle differences in colour or shade to spot prey. Mammals augment their eyesight with highly developed senses of smell and hearing to help them locate distant or concealed food. Finely tuned senses also help prey animals. Just as carnivores pick up the scent of prey before they can see it, so herbivores can detect predators before they come into view. This battle of the senses has led to the evolution of countering forms of behaviour, such as predators moving downwind of their prey when stalking it to prevent their own scent from being picked up.

GREY WOLF

HIGHLY EVOLVED

SENSES, GREAT STAMINA AND THE ABILITY TO LIVE AND HUNT AS A GROUP have made the grey wolf into an evolutionary success story. At one time it was the dominant predator across most of the Northern Hemisphere, from Canada to Siberia, from the Arctic to India. Mainly because of human activity, it has now disappeared from much of its former range, but it survives where wilderness dominates in northern Canada, Russia and around the Arctic.

A social animal, the grey wolf lives and hunts in packs dominated by a single breeding pair. Pack size varies and is largely dependent on the size of prey most commonly found in its range. In areas where moose are the main target, packs may number as many as 20 individuals. Smaller deer require fewer animals to overpower them, and where these are the main prey packs tend to number around seven.

The grey wolf has excellent sight and hearing, but its most highly developed sense is that of smell. It has a long nose filled with billions of scent receptors, and can locate prey using smell alone – a vital asset in the wilderness areas that are its home.

ORDER: Carnivora
FAMILY: Canidae
HABITAT: Forests, plains, deserts, tundra and mountains
DIET: Meat
MAXIMUM LENGTH: 2 m
MAXIMUM WEIGHT: 80 kg
DISTRIBUTION: Northern Russia, Canada and the Arctic

VITAL STATISTICS

MATING GAMES

IN THE COMPETITION TO PASS ON GENES, THE ABILITY TO ATTRACT A MATE IS VITAL. This evolutionary pressure has led to many of the most spectacular sights and sounds in the animal kingdom, from the peacock's tail and the courtship dances of birds of paradise to the song of the humpback whale. Success in mating is all about beating the competition. In most animal species, the females choose their partners and the males compete for the right to mate. There is a good reason for this: males produce huge numbers of sex cells, or sperm, and have the potential to father offspring with many females during a breeding season at no extra cost to themselves. Females, on the other hand, need to be choosy. Their eggs are fewer, larger and take a lot more energy to produce than sperm do.

Once mated, most female birds and land animals carry their eggs or young around with them until they are ready to be laid or born. Because of the time this takes, a female needs to choose the strongest, fittest father to ensure that her young receive the genes most likely to improve their chances of survival – and their own chances of mating later on. In many species, females get only one shot at this during each breeding season, unlike males, who have the possibility of fathering several offspring with different females.

Competition for mates in the animal kingdom takes various forms. The vicious battles fought by some males are spectacular but dangerous and are extreme ways of securing the right to mate. Many animals avoid physical contact and instead use display to secure the attention of females. This is particularly common among species of bird. Males are often brightly coloured or have showy feathers to catch a female's eye.

Dressed to impress

Bright colours and ornate feathers can tell a female a great deal about a male's fitness and his suitability as a mate. Gaudy feathers take a lot of energy to produce and maintain, and males in poor condition are outshone by fitter ones. In order to attract females, some male birds grow feathers that are unusually long. The symmetry of these feathers is also important. Male swallows, for instance, have long, forked tails. Females tend to prefer males with longer tail feathers, but they will choose a male with a shorter but symmetrical tail over a one whose tail is noticeably longer on one side than the other.

This selection of male birds by females on the basis of their feathers is a strong driver for evolutionary change. In species where length and symmetry are important, males with shorter, less symmetrical feathers are much less likely to mate, so their genes rarely make it into the next generation. The result is that over time the feathers that make a difference – usually tail feathers – tend to become longer and more symmetrical throughout all the males of the species. This can result in extremes. The male Reeves's pheasant from China, for instance, has central tail feathers that can exceed 2.4 m long – the longest feathers of any wild bird. Those of the female, by contrast, rarely exceed 30 cm in length.

The colours of the male and female Reeves's pheasant also reflect the different purposes that their feathers fulfill. The male has a handsome collar of iridescent green and, farther down his body, white feathers edged with black. These make him stand out like a jewel in the dense foliage of the forests where he lives. The female has mottled brown plumage that has evolved for camouflage, helping her to avoid the attentions of predators, particularly when she is nesting on the forest floor.

The quality of a male's feathers is often enhanced by movements designed to show them off to best effect. The peacock spreads out his tail feathers like a fan. Other birds, such as South America's cock-of-the-rock, perform a dance. Both the feathers and the behaviour evolved as a result of natural selection. In this case, the selective pressure was applied from within the species, by female choice, rather than from predators or changes in the environment.

PUSH AND SHOVE A group of male red-sided garter snakes compete for the larger female by trying to push each other out of the way.

Visual signals among birds do not always take the form of feathers. The male magnificent frigatebird, for example, has a large red throat pouch, which he inflates to attract a passing female to his nest. Magnificent frigatebirds nest in colonies, so the females have plenty of males to choose from. Exactly what it is that makes them settle for one male over another is unclear. It could be the size of the pouch, its symmetry or the intensity of its colour. More than likely, it is a combination of all three.

Sensory attractions

Many birds use visual signals to select a mate because sight is their most highly developed sense. Other animals, which rely on different senses, attract mates in different ways. Male frogs, for example, often attract mates with sound. Each species has its own unique call to ensure that they attract females of their own kind. Large frogs make deeper calls than small ones. This difference in tone may help females to decide which males to head towards as potential partners.

Many mammals, particularly those that live solitary lives in densely vegetated places such as forests, attract mates with scent. Such creatures include tigers and other wild species of cat. Among these mammals, females do not choose mates; rather, they have mates imposed on them. Dominant males maintain and defend large territories that encompass the smaller ranges of several females. These males mate with all the females in their territory. They regularly check the scent marks left by females, which tell them when an individual is ready to mate. The males also make scent marks, but these are distributed around the borders of their territory and serve to tell other males that the territory is occupied. Scent, both to attract mates and to defend

TEST OF STRENGTH Male moose fight by pushing each other with their antlers. The strongest wins the right to mate, and may mate with several females each year.

territories, may be backed up with sound. Female tigers roar to announce their readiness to mate, while males roar to warn rival males to stay away.

Fighting

The most obvious form of competition for mates is the direct test of strength. In some animals, males try to push rivals off females in order to mate with them. This behaviour is seen in some snakes, with the females, which tend to be larger, surrounded by struggling suitors. However, in most species that do not use display, males fight on a one-to-one basis for access to females.

Fighting, by its nature, is a dangerous activity and most males tend to avoid it unless it is absolutely necessary, even in the breeding season. Rival males size one another up before going into battle. If one is clearly smaller or weaker than the other, he will usually retreat. Only when two animals are closely matched do they actually fight, and even then the battles are usually designed to avoid injury. Hoofed mammals lock horns or antlers and wrestle to determine which is the stronger, or, in the case of goats or sheep, clash their heads together until one participant backs down or gives up. Male elephants lock tusks and go head to head in similar tests of strength.

Fights for mates are usually bloodless, but there are exceptions. Animals that are naturally aggressive may injure or even kill one another in the battle to breed. For lions, control of a pride is the only chance they will ever have of siring young, and a lion ousted from a pride will never breed again. What is more, if his pride is taken over, any of his cubs that are too small to run away will be killed by the new dominant male or males. If a lion is to pass on his genes, he must hold on to a pride whatever the risk, even if it means a fight to the death.

Controlling interest

In some cases, mate choice has less to do with the quality of the male than with what he can offer. A good, large territory that is rich in food for raising young swings the decision for many females. In many species, males do not fight for females but

rather for space. Having secured a good site for themselves, these males declare ownership of their territory with clear messages. Birds sing to advertise their ownership of an area, while many mammals scent-mark around the borders of their personal territory.

These messages tell other males that an area is occupied, and they may also impart more detailed information. The volume and complexity of bird song, together with the frequency and length of the bursts, tells other males a great deal about the strength and experience of the bird producing it, for instance. Other males in the vicinity can then decide how to act on the information, whether to treat it as a warning to steer clear (if the current occupant is stronger) or as an invitation to attack.

BEACH BATTLE Elephant seal bulls engage in aggressive fights to establish territory and mating rights. Dominant bulls may acquire a harem of up to 50 females.

PARENTAL CARE

EVERYTHING A PARENT DOES REGARDING ITS OFFSPRING IS AN EVOLUTIONARY RESPONSE designed to improve the offspring's chances of survival and, by doing so, to increase the chance of the parent's genes continuing into the future.

Parental care varies from the most simple and seemingly inconsequential acts to months or years of providing food, while also acting as teacher and bodyguard. At its most basic, it is exhibited by creatures that hide their eggs. This small act takes little energy, but can make a great difference to the proportion of eggs that survive until hatching. Many fish that spawn over the bottom use a simple wriggle or a swish of the tail to cover their eggs in sediment, which is enough to hide the eggs from creatures that might eat them. Fish that conceal their young in this way have much higher hatching success rates than those that do not.

Many reptiles also conceal their eggs. Marine turtles come ashore to lay their eggs on beaches, burying them in the sand. Most do this at night to reduce the chance of birds and other predators snatching eggs before they can be covered. Alligators and

CARE ON THE MOVE The female mantis shrimp produces thousands of eggs, which she cleans and turns until they hatch.

FOOD SUPPLY Flamingos feed their newly hatched young on a liquid secreted in the digestive tracts of both males and females. After about two months, the chicks' bills have developed enough for them to filter feed for themselves.

FACTS

THE EGGS OF THE ROYAL ALBATROSS TAKE 78-81 DAYS TO INCUBATE, the longest of any flying bird, and parents feed their chick for seven to eight months. Pairs stay faithful for life – essential when young take so long to raise.

JUST FOUR DAYS AFTER BEING BORN, HOODED SEAL PUPS are weaned. This is the shortest weaning period known in mammals, and it enables the pups to take to the sea as quickly as possible.

FACTS

OSTRICH

ONE OF THE BEST PARENTS

IN THE NATURAL WORLD is the male ostrich. A male mates with several females, all of which lay their eggs in one nest. He not only incubates the eggs – which may number up to 40 – with the help of the dominant female, but also looks after the chicks until they are big enough to fend for themselves against predators such as jackals and hawks.

The ostrich is found in open habitat throughout southern Africa, and is well adapted for survival there. It has the largest eyes of any land vertebrate (50 mm across). Its acute eyesight and hearing enable it to detect predators a long way off. Its long legs make it pacy enough to outrun most predators – with a top speed of 72 km/h, it is the fastest running bird on the planet – and if it finds itself cornered or its chicks are threatened, it can lash out violently with the fearsome, pickaxe-like claw on each foot. It also lays the biggest eggs of any bird species, containing as much yolk and white as two dozen hens' eggs.

If two males with broods meet each other, they may fight. If one is driven off, his young attach themselves to the victor. The winning father accepts this, possibly because it may reduce the chances of members of his own brood being taken by predators. Some males end up looking after as many as 60 youngsters from different broods.

VITAL STATISTICS

ORDER: Struthioniformes (ratites)
FAMILY: Struthionidae
SPECIES: *Struthio camelus*
HABITAT: Savannah, scrub and semi-desert
DISTRIBUTION: Southern Africa
DIET: Leaves and other vegetation, and small animals such as lizards
KEY FEATURES: Long legs; large eyes; does not need to drink

EATING AND FEEDING A female pig can suckle several young and feed herself at the same time.

some crocodiles construct nests in mounds of vegetation, or dig a shallow pit, in which to conceal their eggs. Unlike turtles, which abandon their buried eggs after laying, these reptiles often stand guard.

Nest-building and protection

The greatest nest-builders in the animal kingdom are birds. Unlike most reptiles, birds sit on their eggs to incubate them. This behaviour probably evolved as a means to speed up the time it took for eggs to hatch. Egg incubation is time-consuming and leaves the sitter unable to feed, and in most bird species, adults develop strong pair bonds, with one partner bringing back food while the other sits on the nest. Many birds feed their chicks when they have hatched, and even for a while after they have fledged. Young birds usually stay with their parents for some time after leaving the nest, learning what to eat and how to find it, and receiving protection from their parents, who drive off predators or divert their attention from the young.

Some fish are nearly as doting over their offspring as birds, building nests and caring for the young after they have hatched. In some species, the male guards the eggs. If the water is stagnant, he may fan the eggs with his fins to improve the flow of water over them and increase the amount of oxygen they receive. Fish that behave in this way include the sticklebacks and many less well-known species. Some species go one step further, using their mouths and gill cavities as mobile nests. This mouth-brooding behaviour is common among cichlids and is usually carried out by the male. Even when the fry have hatched, they usually stay with their father and use his mouth as a place of refuge until they are big enough to fend for themselves.

Nourishment and nurture

The ultimate parental care-givers are the mammals, the vast majority of which give birth to live young. Mammals are defined by the parental care they provide. They are the only animals that produce milk for their young – a super-concentrated liquid food produced by specialised glands and expressed through the skin. The time young mammals spend with their parents (usually their mother) varies from species to species. Those that spend longer, particularly after they are weaned, tend to be those that have the most to learn about survival. Most carnivores, for instance, stay with their mother or the family group for at least a year, often longer, as hunting is a skill that takes time to learn.

THE OTHER OPTION

Creatures that care for their young are limited in the number that they can successfully raise. This strategy, known as K-selection, is used by species that live in crowded but stable environments. Many animals and most plants adopt an alternative strategy – known as r-selection – producing as many offspring (or seeds) as possible and leaving them to fend for themselves. These organisms live in unstable or unpredictable conditions where the ability to reproduce quickly is vital, and include many invertebrates, particularly those that live their lives attached to one spot or unable to move very far, such as corals (below) and shellfish. Among vertebrates, this strategy is most common in amphibians and fish.

ADAPTING TO CHANGE

ENVIRONMENTAL CHANGE IS THE MAIN REASON NEW SPECIES EVOLVE. The battles between predators and prey and the struggle to breed have modified animals, but rarely to the extent that the animals alter enough to become new species. A change of surroundings can force animals to change more radically if they are not to die out completely.

One species that is currently under serious threat from environmental change is the polar bear. Yet, it is itself a relatively new species – newer, in fact, than our own – having evolved some time between 100 000 and 250 000 years ago. Its existence to date is a mere heartbeat in the history of life on Earth. The polar bear evolved from the brown bear (also known as the grizzly in North America), and a superb fossil record traces the intermediate stages between the two species.

This new species, the polar bear, had not just changed its coat from that of its ancestors – its skull was longer and it had lost all of its molar teeth, leaving only those useful for its new, entirely carnivorous diet.

Polar bears evolved from a relatively small population of brown bears that became cut off from their normal habitat by ice at the beginning of one of the Earth's many ice ages. Many of the brown bears perished, but cubs that were born with lighter coloured, thicker coats than their parents survived. (Coat variation is common within litters of brown bears even today.) These paler, shaggier cubs were both better camouflaged against their new surroundings and better insulated from the cold. They were pre-adapted, through natural variation, to cope with the changing climate better than their siblings. When they grew up and bred with similar bears, some of their cubs had even paler, thicker coats. With each generation, the population of bears subtly changed. Over thousands of generations a new species appeared, which spread throughout the Arctic. This new species, the polar bear, had not just changed its coat; it differed from its ancestors in other ways, too. Its skull was longer and it had lost all of its molar teeth, leaving only those useful for its new, entirely carnivorous diet.

Throughout the Earth's history, climate change has had a massive impact on the evolution of life. When the Earth's climate alters, it does more than just cool or warm the air, sea and land. Snow and ice, or the lack of them, turn everything a different colour. Food sources and landscapes change as trees and other plants flourish or disappear.

Just as the onset of past ice ages has driven the evolution of new species that still share the planet with us today, so the disappearance of ice sheets that covered large areas of land has led to other species dying out. Some of these, such as the woolly mammoth, have only relatively recently become extinct. With thick coats and heavy layers of fat, and long tusks for digging in the snow, the mammoth was well adapted to surviving in freezing conditions, but was probably unable to adapt to the warmer conditions prevalent after the ice age ended. Most died out 12 000 years ago, but small populations survived in the Arctic until as recently as 4000 BC. When the ice returns again, as it will, yet more new species will evolve. As long as conditions on Earth are subject to change, so are its flora and fauna.

Breaking new ground

The conditions an animal finds itself in can change much more quickly than the planet's climate. Creatures blown in or washed up on islands and other isolated land masses are apt to find themselves in a world very different from the one they are used to. As with climate change, they are often forced to adapt quickly in order to survive. The marine iguanas of the Galápagos are one example of rapid adaptation to a new environment.

CHANGE OF DIET Marine iguanas of the Galápagos Islands feed exclusively on algae, which they graze from submerged rocks near the shore. This was the only plant food available to their ancestors, washed up here from mainland South America.

ADAPT OR DISAPPEAR The polar bear evolved during the onset of a past ice age, but the species is now threatened by global warming and the melting of the Arctic ice.

Evolution and the Galápagos have a famous historical link, of course. It was after visiting the islands, some 1000 km west of Ecuador in the Pacific Ocean, that Charles Darwin began putting his theory of evolution by natural selection down on paper. Darwin was inspired by the array of creatures he saw on the islands. Many of them were clearly related to animals from the South American mainland, but they differed in ways that were often quite profound.

One of the strangest animals Darwin saw was the marine iguana. In South America, iguanas are common lizards of forest and woodland. They feed on fruit and other vegetable matter, and normally live alone. The marine iguanas of the Galápagos, on the other hand, live in groups by the sea. They feed entirely on algae in the sea and dive beneath the waves to get it or graze at low tide.

Although Darwin did not himself make the link, other scientists later realised that marine iguanas had not always lived that way. Their strange lifestyle is the evolutionary result of vegetarian land lizards being washed up on volcanic islands which had limited plant life. The algae growing in profusion on rocks near the shore provided an untapped food resource that their ancestors were able to eat. Over the generations they

ABSENCE OF MAMMALS The kiwi has evolved to hunt like a mammal on the forest floor, using its sense of smell to find food.

monopolised it, and their bodies and behaviour changed as they adapted to harvest the food supply more efficiently. In doing so, they changed into a completely new species.

Filling a gap

Wherever they live in the world, most animals have evolved to fill a particular niche. Some species are generalists – and on the whole these creatures are quite successful – but the majority are not so much jacks of all trades as masters of one. Creatures arriving on islands or moving into habitats where there is little competition tend to evolve to fill niches that they find vacant, and this leads to highly specialised adaptations. The rain forests of Australia and New Guinea, for instance, lack monkeys, which elsewhere have monopolised the fruit- and leaf-eating niches high up in the trees. Instead, these rain forests are inhabited by tree kangaroos, which have evolved to climb and live in the trees. Compared to monkeys, tree kangaroos move through the trees in a slow and rather ungainly way, but with no competition for food they are as agile as they need to be.

Tree kangaroos evolved from kangaroos that lived on the ground, and they have retained some of their ancestor's characteristics. Their back legs are shorter than those of ground-dwelling kangaroos, but they are still longer than their front legs. Unlike their ground-dwelling cousins, tree kangaroos can move their back legs independently of each other, enabling them to climb. They can also hop from branch to branch while balancing with their elongated, flexible tails. Researchers think that tree kangaroos appeared quite recently, perhaps as little as 5 million years ago. Evolution being what it is, it is likely that descendants of today's tree kangaroos will be better adapted for life in the branches. It is possible that in the distant future, today's tree kangaroos will be considered an intermediate evolutionary stage.

Species that evolved longer ago seem far better adapted to the niches they occupy. In New Zealand, types of habitat that

A REMNANT POPULATION OF WOOLLY MAMMOTHS

on Siberia's Wrangel Island lived on after the end of the last ice age, when most woolly mammoths disappeared. They became dwarfs to suit their smaller home and survived until about 4000 years ago – around the time the Egyptian pyramids were being built.

HEDGEHOGS
HAVE ALTERED THEIR DIET
on the Scottish island of Uist. Since they were introduced in 1974, they have turned from their usual food of slugs to plunder birds' eggs, and are considered a serious pest.

elsewhere are filled by mammals are instead occupied by birds. Long isolated, New Zealand has no native mammals apart from bats, but birds, being able to fly, had no difficulty colonising its two islands. With an abundance of food on the forest floor and no mammals to prey on them, some species took to living on the ground, and several eventually became flightless. The bird most often associated with New Zealand, the kiwi, is among the most highly evolved of these colonists.

Except for its bill, the kiwi is about as unbirdlike as a bird can get. It has thick, stubby legs, a rounded body and feathers like hair. It even appears to have whiskers. The kiwi's resemblance to a mammal is more than coincidence, it is an example of convergent evolution. It looks like a small forest-floor mammal because it lives in the same way as one. It spends the daylight hours in a burrow, and at night it hunts invertebrates in the leaf litter and soft forest soil, using smell to locate its prey – like a mammal. The nostrils at the tip of its bill are so sensitive it can sniff out worms as it probes the soil. If startled it runs for cover, and then sniffs the air to see if the danger has gone.

Disadvantages of isolation

The kiwi is just one of the birds in New Zealand that has evolved to fill niches normally occupied by other groups. Another is the kakapo, the world's largest parrot. This lumbering creature has also become flightless and spends most of its time on the forest floor. Unlike the kiwi, it is vegetarian, feeding on leaves, tubers and fallen fruit. The niche the kakapo fills would elsewhere be occupied by deer, rodents or other forest mammals. Unlike these creatures, the kakapo evolved in the absence of predators. With no danger to escape from, it gradually lost the natural wariness of plant-eaters and became easy to approach. This change in its behaviour has been its downfall. Since Europeans arrived in New Zealand, the kakapo has all but disappeared. The world's largest parrot was not hunted by people, but by their pets and other introduced mammals, such as stoats and rats.

The story of island species being driven to extinction by introduced predators and competitors is a familiar one. The lost species is always at the centre of the story, with the introduced one cast as villain, but the introduced animals are just doing what comes naturally to them. In evolutionary terms, they are successes, adapting quickly to their new environment.

UNLIKELY CLIMBER Like all tree kangaroos, Matschie's tree kangaroo of New Guinea has developed long, strong claws and muscular forelimbs for climbing and a long tail for balance. It can also leap up to 9 m through the branches.

OUT OF THE RACE

LATEST VICTIM In 2006, the Yangtze River dolphin – 'the goddess of the Yangtze' – was declared extinct. At 20 million years old it was one of the world's most ancient mammal species, and is the first recorded loss of a cetacean species due to human activity.

EVOLUTION HAS WINNERS AND LOSERS. Some species are able to adapt to change and survive. Others fall by the wayside and disappear forever. Extinction is a natural part of the evolutionary process. As organisms evolve over time, they change in structure and form. Most of the animals alive on Earth today are directly descended from other creatures that looked so different from them that we would consider them different species. The exact point at which one species turns into another is impossible to define. The process is slow and gradual, with countless intermediate stages.

In a way, extinct organisms that have living descendants are not really extinct at all: they still exist, but in a greatly altered form. Most of us would consider the early hominid *Australopithecus afarensis* to be extinct – there are none wandering the Earth today. Yet, if that species was our direct ancestor – and there is a lot of evidence to suggest that it was – it is not actually extinct, it lives on in us.

Loss and gain

Nowadays, our own species is the main cause of extinctions on Earth. The extinctions we have caused are complete – rather than forcing organisms to change in order to survive, we have wiped them out utterly. However, we are not the only organisms to bring about the total extinction of other species – many other animals have done so in the past. Soon after the land bridge formed between the continents of North and South America, around 3 million years ago, numerous species in South America, in

Natural catastrophes on a global scale have wiped out vast swathes of species, including entire orders of animals and plants. Yet just as these events caused choas and ended great lineages of life, so they also opened up new opportunities and stimulated new life forms to evolve.

16 119 SPECIES OF ANIMALS AND PLANTS were classified as facing extinction in the World Conservation Union's biennial Red List published in 2006. This included one in eight of all birds, one in four mammals and one in three amphibians.

FACTS

80 YEARS after being discovered on Mauritius by Europeans, in around 1600, the dodo was extinct. A flightless bird, it was hunted into oblivion for food.

99 PER CENT OF ALL THE SPECIES THAT HAVE ever existed on the Earth are now extinct.

FACTS

particular, became extinct. Whole groups of species disappeared, wiped out by new predators or overwhelmed by the arrival of more efficient competitors for food and resources. Many of the extinctions caused by humans have been brought about in the same way. As we have spread around the globe, we have been the new super-efficient predators or competitors for resources.

The spread of humanity has caused extinctions indirectly, too. Wherever we have travelled, we have taken animals with us. Pets such as cats and stowaways such as rats are now almost as widespread as we are. In many cases, the arrival of non-native species has proved disastrous for the indigenous fauna. Species on islands have been particularly vulnerable, many having evolved in the absence of land predators. Even without alien invaders, island species are at greater risk of extinction than other species as their natural range is so small. A volcanic eruption, tsunami or other natural disaster can wipe out the entire global population of an island species in a flash.

Looking back through Earth's history, natural disasters have possibly been the single biggest cause of extinctions. The greatest of these catastrophes, occurring on a global scale,

wiped out vast swathes of species, including entire orders of animals and plants. Yet, just as these events caused chaos and ended great lineages of life, so they also opened up new opportunities and stimulated new life forms to evolve. The catastrophe at the end of the Cretaceous period, thought to have been caused by a massive asteroid impact, wiped out the dinosaurs but cleared the way for mammals to radiate and evolve new forms. While extinction might seem disastrous, in the long term it is just part of the great ongoing story of life on Earth. In fact, were it not for extinction, our own species would not exist.

EVIDENCE
CHANGE

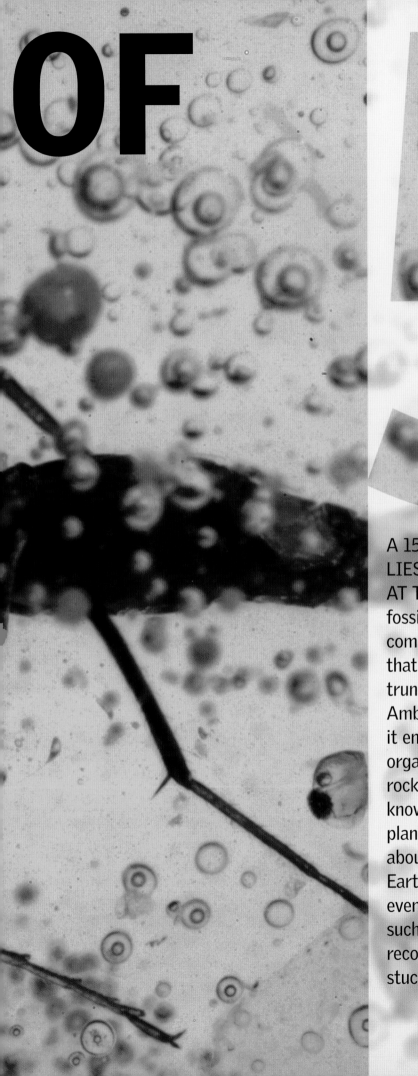

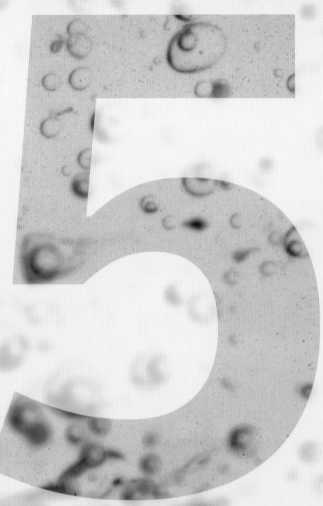

A 15-MILLION-YEAR-OLD PRAYING MANTIS LIES TRAPPED IN AMBER, FROZEN IN TIME AT THE POINT OF DEATH. Amber is the fossilised sap of conifer trees and a relatively common semi-precious stone. The processes that formed it continue today: sap oozes down trunks, hits the ground and is eventually buried. Amber preserves any small animals and plants it envelops in perfect detail, but far more organisms become fossilised in sedimentary rock. Together, these remains tell us all that we know about the living things that inhabited the planet before our time. Fossils also offer clues about the dynamic forces that have shaped Earth's history, including numerous extinction events that have wiped out many life forms, such as the dinosaurs. Without this fossil record our knowledge of life on Earth would be stuck in the present.

SET IN STONE

THE REASON THAT WE KNOW AS MUCH AS WE DO ABOUT THE ORGANISMS THAT LIVED ON EARTH BEFORE US is because their remains have been preserved and left behind in rocks as fossils. Usually nothing, or very little, of the original organism remains, its tissues having been replaced by inorganic materials. Only very rarely is biological material preserved intact and then usually from fossils that have been formed fairly recently. Creatures trapped in amber – formed from the sticky resin which oozes from pine trees – are the most exquisitely preserved, but amber more than 30 million years old is uncommon. Even in amber, body tissues decay and older amber fossils usually contain only chitin – a substance found in the exoskeleton (outer skeleton) of insects and other arthropods.

Hard evidence

While most fossils lack their original biological material, they are still able to tell us a great deal about the organisms that originally formed them. Flesh and skin rarely fossilise in rock but bones, teeth, shells and other hard tissues are common. Teeth can tell us instantly what an animal ate. Long, sharp teeth for stabbing or slicing indicate that the animal that owned them was a meat-eater. Simple, peg-like teeth and teeth with large, flattened surfaces for grinding suggest a diet of plants. Teeth are also a good indicator of the relatedness of fossil animals to animals alive today. Many of the earliest mammals are known only from their teeth – tooth enamel is incredibly tough and more likely to fossilise than bone, especially the delicate bones of small animals. Sharks and other fish with skeletons of cartilage rather than bone are also principally known from tooth fossils.

Shells often provide the only record of invertebrate animals. Lacking bones and teeth, invertebrates without shells very rarely fossilise well. By comparing fossilised shells with those of living

Careful study of the preserved body parts led scientists to the conclusion that *Scipionyx* was a fast-moving, powerful predator – a 'turbocharged reptile'.

THEN AND NOW *As well as showing change, fossils bear witness to stability. Some organisms, such as this darter dragonfly (left), have barely altered since their ancestors first appeared on Earth. The fossil dragonfly above flew in a world populated by dinosaurs, more than 100 million years ago.*

animals, we know, for instance, that many molluscs have barely changed in more than 100 million years. Shells are also the only record we have for many long extinct animal groups.

An exceptional find

The reason that soft tissues rarely fossilise is that they quickly rot or are eaten by scavengers. Under exceptional circumstances, however, they are sometimes preserved. If an animal's body is covered quickly enough by sediment in which oxygen levels are low, there is a chance that its muscles and internal organs might not only be entombed but also preserved long enough for that sediment to become rock. When that happens there is a possibility they may turn into fossils.

Good soft tissue fossils are so rare that when they are found their discovery can cause a sensation. In 1999, the unearthing of a small dinosaur fossil in southern Italy did just that. The fossil, found in rocks dated at 110 million years old, was of a baby meat-eating dinosaur known as *Scipionyx*. As well as bones, the fossil revealed parts of the dinosaur's liver, large intestine, windpipe and muscles – structures that had never been seen in such detail in a meat-eating dinosaur fossil before. Careful study of these preserved body parts, and comparison with those of living animals, led scientists to the conclusion that *Scipionyx* was a fast-moving, powerful predator – a 'turbocharged reptile', according to one palaeontologist. It was further evidence that dinosaurs were not the sluggish, lumbering creatures they were once thought to be.

HOW FOSSILS FORM

Fossils are only found in sedimentary rocks. Palaeontologists search for them in areas where ancient sedimentary rocks have been brought to the surface by movements in the Earth's crust or exposed by erosion. Sedimentary rocks form from sand, silt and mud that build up at the bottom of bodies of water. As more and more sediment is laid down, the layers underneath are compressed. This compression, together with chemical reactions between the grains, causes the layers of sediment to solidify and turn into rock. Fossils are the remains of animals and other organisms that sink to the bottom and are then covered by sediment. As they are buried they, too, are compressed, but they are not crushed completely: the rock forms around them. Over time the chemicals within the remains alter as water infused with minerals seeps through the rock. Eventually, these minerals replace the bone or other organic tissues completely, filling the space they created in the rock with a mineral facsimile, like a plaster cast. Most fossils found in rock are completely mineralised. Only those of organisms that were buried relatively recently in geological time retain any of their original complex organic chemicals, although some older fossils may contain large amounts of the carbon that was contained in them.

TRACKS AND TRACES

FOSSILS NOT ONLY PRESERVE THE BODIES OF ANIMALS, THEY ALSO RECORD OTHER EVIDENCE that helps us to build a fuller picture of how creatures that are now extinct once lived. Footprints, burrows and droppings, for instance, have all been preserved in rocks. Known as 'trace fossils', they are literally traces of long-distant lives.

Fossils of all kinds are far more rare than one might first imagine. The reason for this is that they form only under certain conditions. The vast majority of animals, plants and other organisms that lived in the past were never fossilised. Most were either eaten or rotted away after death in places where fossils could not form – on land, for example, or on rocky or shingle beds in rivers, lakes and seas. Trace fossils are even rarer than true fossils of bones, shells and teeth. Traces are far more ephemeral: footprints, burrows and even droppings rarely last as long as bones and other solid structures. In order to be preserved at all they must be covered by sediment quickly.

Footprints and trackways provide an extra insight into how extinct animals lived. Somehow, a dinosaur's footprint in the rock seems more immediate than a collection of its fossilised bones. It is concrete evidence that the animal once lived, breathed and roamed the Earth.

Footprints were not only made by dinosaurs, of course: many other extinct creatures have left them behind. The earliest evidence of animal life on land is footprints that were left in mud. The small invertebrate animals that made them left no fossils of their bodies behind – at least, none that have been found or recognised so far. Unless such fossils are found, the exact identity of these creatures will remain a mystery. So we might never know what they were, but we do know that they were here.

Burrows, like footprints, are often enigmatic trace fossils. The vast majority were created by marine worms or similar creatures. Again, they tell us that life existed in certain places at certain times but they do not give us any great detail as to what that life looked like.

Ancient droppings

On the other hand, the study of coprolites, as fossilised droppings are known (from the Greek word *kopros*, meaning dung), can be surprisingly revealing and provide an invaluable picture of a creature's diet and environment. The largest coprolite ever found was discovered in Saskatchewan, Canada, in 1995. Its size – 42 cm long – age and location led scientists to conclude that it had been made by a *Tyrannosaurus rex*. Further study showed that the dropping contained many splinters of bone.

GIANT STEPS These three-toed footprints in rocks near Denver, Colorado, were made by a close relative of the plant-eating Iguanodon. *Extensive trackways of such prints have been found in the region. They include the impressions of feet both large and small, suggesting a migrating herd containing both adults and youngsters.*

This proved that *Tyrannosaurus rex* not only sliced flesh from its prey but crushed its bonesand ate them, too.

Fossilised eggs

Fossil eggs also cast a revealing light on prehistoric life. Dinosaur eggs, for example, are often found in groups, sometimes arranged in particular patterns. These strongly suggest that dinosaurs nested, as birds do today. Rare fossils have even shown dinosaur nests with young hatchlings. One plant-eating dinosaur, known as *Maiasaura*, appears to have brought food to its young at the nest. Close examination of the nestling babies showed that their legs were not fully developed, so they would not have been able to find food for themselves. These same babies also show the first signs of wear to their teeth – evidence that they were not newly hatched when they were buried and fossilised, but had already begun feeding.

BIG BONED *True fossils, as opposed to trace fossils, include dinosaur bones. This massive femur (thigh bone) belonged to an* Apatosaurus, *a long-necked, plant-eating dinosaur that lived around 140 million years ago.*

CLUES TO CLIMATE

IN ADDITION TO A WEALTH OF INFORMATION ON THE ANIMALS AND PLANTS THAT ONCE LIVED ON EARTH, FOSSILS ALSO GIVE US A GOOD INDICATION OF CLIMATE. By looking at the types of animals and plants that lived in particular places in the Earth's past, we can make an educated guess as to what the climate was like in those places at that time. Coal deposits, for instance, have been found on every one of the continents, including Antarctica. Coal is the fossilised remains of wood from swampy forests. The fact that most of the world's coal was laid down during a particular time in the Earth's history – the Carboniferous period, which lasted from 360 to 286 million years ago – tells us that the planet's atmosphere at that time was much more humid than it is today.

Just as coal deposits indicate moist conditions, so other plant fossils indicate, or at least suggest, drought. As the Carboniferous period ends and the next period, the Permian, begins, coal deposits quickly disappear from sedimentary rocks, and along with them go most of the moisture-loving amphibians. In their place we find more and more fossils of a new group of animals, the reptiles – creatures adapted to breed on land and survive for long periods without water.

Other clues back up the idea that the Earth was drying out at this time. Evaporites (such as halite, or rock salt) are found in ever increasing concentrations during the Permian, as are similar deposits known as calcretes. Evaporites form on the surface as bodies of water are evaporated under hot, dry conditions. Modern evaporite deposits include the salt pans of Arizona in the USA. Calcretes are caused by the build-up of minerals within the soil by evaporation rather than on top of it, forming a hard crust which often cracks in the sun.

Evaporites and calcretes, like coal, give a general picture of what the climate was like in the area where they formed. Some other minerals give more specific information. Ikaite, for instance, is a rare mineral that occurs in alkaline, phosphate-rich marine and continental waters at temperatures up to 7°C. It derives its name from the Ikka Fjord in Greenland, where there are hundreds of ikaite column formations. Because it forms only under very specific conditions, its occurrence in ancient rocks is a marker for those conditions having existed in the past.

Other clues to climate come from the concentrations of certain isotopes of chemical elements within rocks. Elements such as sulphur, carbon and oxygen can occur in slightly different forms, each of which is created under different conditions. One particular isotope of sulphur, for instance, is created only by volcanic activity. Large amounts of this isotope in rocks tells scientists that there was a great deal of volcanic activity.on the Earth when those rocks were laid down.

Knowing what gases there were in the atmosphere at various times in the Earth's history is one of the best indicators of ancient climates. High concentrations of the greenhouse gases carbon dioxide and methane, for example – both of which can be deduced from the composition of sedimentary rocks – indicate that the Earth was almost certainly hotter when those rocks were formed than it is today.

FROZEN IN TIME Researchers examine an ancient bed of moss in the McMurdo Dry Valleys, a relatively ice-free region of Antarctica. The moss is believed to be 13 million years old and is not fossilised but freeze-dried. Its existence is evidence that Antarctica was warmer in the past.

COLUMN GARDEN A diver examines one of the remarkable ikaite columns which grow like stalagmites from the bottom of the Ikka Fjord in south-west Greenland. Over 700 of the submarine columns – some up to 20 m high – have been mapped over a 2 km stretch of the fjord (left).

For most of Earth's history evidence from rocks is the only record available. More recent atmospheres, however, have actually been preserved as bubbles in the icecaps that have formed around the poles. With every year's snowfall the icecaps grow slightly thicker and the layers of snow below become ever more compressed. By drilling down into the icecaps to take core samples, scientists have been able to gain access to preserved bubbles from the atmosphere as far back as 750 000 years.

The dating game

Scientists can accurately determine the age of rocks by examining the decay rates of various radioactive chemical elements – a technique known as radiometric dating. Most radioactive elements are formed by volcanic activity, so this technique is extremely good at dating igneous rocks, such as granite. Radiometric dating can be used to age sedimentary rocks, and hence the fossils within them, but only if certain unusual minerals are present. Glauconite is one such mineral. It contains potassium 40, the radioactive form of potassium, which is created within it as sea-floor sediments are laid down. Where these minerals are not present, sedimentary rocks can be more roughly dated by using the known ages of layers above and below them.

RE-CREATING LOST WORLDS

IN SOME PARTS OF THE WORLD, FOSSIL BEDS HAVE BEEN FOUND THAT ARE SO RICH they give a clear picture of what the ancient habitat would have looked like. One of the richest beds containing early animal life is the Burgess Shale of British Columbia in Canada. Although it now lies high in the Rockies, this was laid down on an area of seabed in the Cambrian period, around 505 million years ago. The Burgess Shale is remarkable partly because of the number of soft-bodied creatures it contains. These normally decay long before they are able to form into fossils, but here they are preserved in

REMARKABLE QUARRY The Solnhofen quarry in Bavaria has long produced high-quality limestone for building. It has also yielded an incredible collection of fossils from the Jurassic period.

*ANCIENT CRUSTACEAN
Many Solnhofen fossils show creatures, such as this prawn, that lived in the lagoon where the limestone formed.*

startling detail. Most of the many animals found here appear to represent lost lineages of invertebrates, which have no living descendants or even close relatives left today.

Other exceptional fossil beds preserve different stages in the history of life. One is the Solnhofen Limestone in Bavaria, Germany, laid down as fine carbonate mud at the bottom of a shallow lagoon near the end of the Jurassic period, around 155 million years ago. It contains a wealth of fossil organisms preserved in exceptional detail. Marine creatures, such as brittle stars and jellyfish, lie alongside dragonflies and other winged insects. Twenty-nine types of pterosaur (winged reptiles) have been discovered, along with several small dinosaurs and early crocodiles.

The most famous creature from the Solnhofen Limestone is the early bird *Archaeopteryx*. The first *Archaeopteryx* fossil ever found was a single, beautifully preserved feather discovered in 1860. This was joined by more complete skeletons, with feather imprints, wing claws and teeth. *Archaeopteryx* remains one of the most important pieces of evidence that birds evolved from dinosaurs. In fact, one of the first *Archaeopteryx* skeletons discovered, which lacked clearly defined feathers, was originally misidentified as a dinosaur.

The variety and detail of the Solnhofen fossils has enabled palaeontologists to re-assemble an entire ecosystem. Leaves and other plant fossils give an idea of the vegetation that grew alongside the lagoon, adding to information about the area's animal inhabitants.

Buried treasure

One of the best-scoured regions for fossils is North America. More prehistoric species are known from this continent than any other. Cretaceous dinosaurs are particularly well represented, including some of the most famous dinosaurs of all, such as *Triceratops* and *Tyrannosaurus rex*. The huge number of Cretaceous fossils from North America have enabled scientists to re-create this place and time in astonishing detail. Paintings, museum dioramas and computer-animated documentaries have all been made using the information collected from these sites.

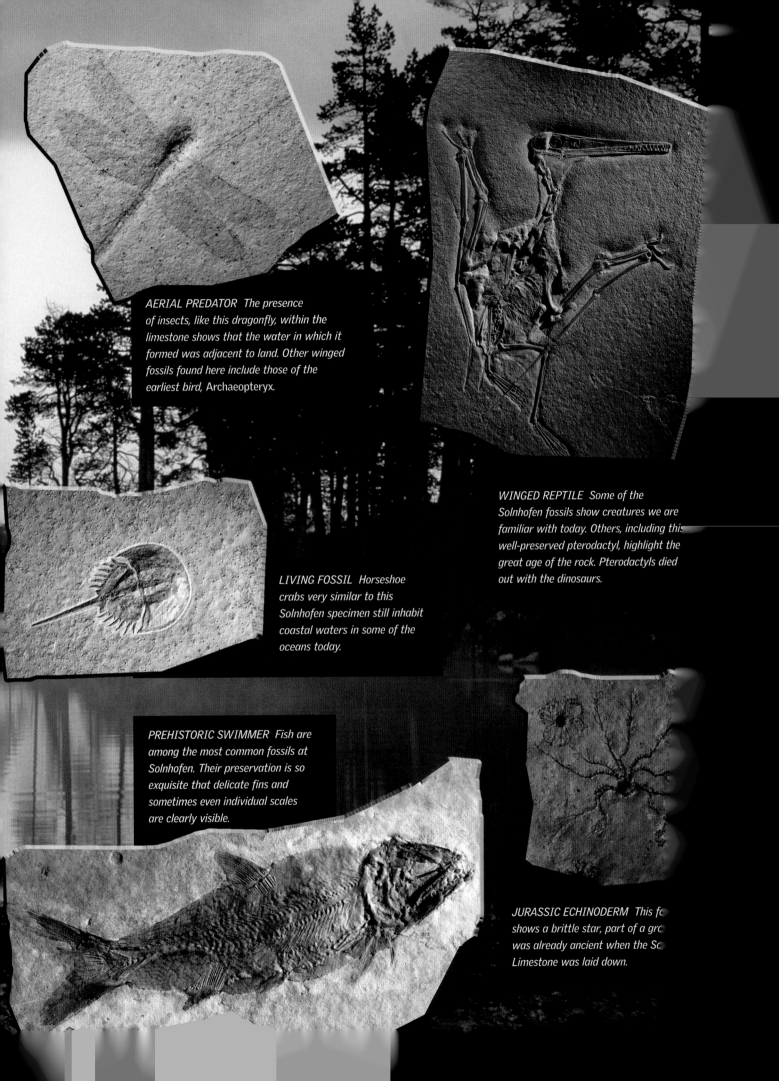

AERIAL PREDATOR The presence of insects, like this dragonfly, within the limestone shows that the water in which it formed was adjacent to land. Other winged fossils found here include those of the earliest bird, Archaeopteryx.

WINGED REPTILE Some of the Solnhofen fossils show creatures we are familiar with today. Others, including this well-preserved pterodactyl, highlight the great age of the rock. Pterodactyls died out with the dinosaurs.

LIVING FOSSIL Horseshoe crabs very similar to this Solnhofen specimen still inhabit coastal waters in some of the oceans today.

PREHISTORIC SWIMMER Fish are among the most common fossils at Solnhofen. Their preservation is so exquisite that delicate fins and sometimes even individual scales are clearly visible.

JURASSIC ECHINODERM This fo shows a brittle star, part of a gro was already ancient when the So Limestone was laid down.

DISASTER
CHAOS

AND 6

SMALL METEORITES HIT THE EARTH EVERY DAY AND EVERY FEW YEARS WE GET A SCARE THAT A BIG ONE MIGHT STRIKE. One day this will surely happen. Around 300 000 years ago a massive meteorite, weighing 50 000 tonnes, hit northern Australia. The result was the Wolfe Creek crater, a vast hole 60 m deep and 800 m wide (left). Where the meteorite struck, the ground melted and the rock beneath boiled. The noise of the explosion would have travelled thousands of miles. The Wolfe Creek impact was recent enough for its crater to remain visible. Other, earlier impacts have been even larger, but their traces are now harder to find. One such strike occurred 65 million years ago at Chicxulub on Mexico's Yucatán Peninsula. It was so vast it caused a mass extinction right around the globe.

MASS EXTINCTIONS

The story of life on Earth has been punctuated by several mass-extinction events. With each event, huge numbers of species disappeared for good. In some, whole families, orders and even classes of life were completely wiped out. Extinction is a natural part of the evolutionary process. When animals or plants die out, new ones evolve to take their place. If the dinosaurs had not been wiped out 65 million years ago, mammals would never have risen to dominance. Mass extinctions have left their imprint in the rocks. Sedimentary rock layers laid down just before each event are rich in fossils. Layers laid down immediately afterwards are virtually fossil-free. Although there have been many mass extinctions, five stand out due to the sheer number of species lost.

END ORDOVICIAN

DURATION	10 million years
EXTINCTIONS	More than 100 families of marine invertebrates, including many bryozoans, conodonts and trilobites
POSSIBLE CAUSE	Global cooling as the supercontinent Gondwanaland moved over the North Pole and became covered by an icecap

BRACHIOPOD FOSSILS
Entire families of brachiopods and other shellfish died out in what was the second worst mass extinction ever.

LATE DEVONIAN

DURATION	20 million years
EXTINCTIONS	Reef-building sponges and corals were the worst affected invertebrate groups. All placoderm armoured fish died out, as did many jawless fish
POSSIBLE CAUSE	Global cooling due to massive glaciation on Gondwanaland

PLACODERM Armoured fish disappeared as the world cooled and sea levels fell.

METEORITES
A meteorite is a rocky or metallic object from space which falls through the atmosphere to strike the Earth's surface. The meteorite thought to have caused the mass extinction that wiped out the dinosaurs crashed into Earth at Chicxulub on the Yucatán Peninsula 65 million years ago. There had been massive meteorite events before, but none as devastating to life on Earth. Measuring 10 km wide, the Chicxulub meteorite blasted a hole 100 km wide and 12 km deep. It is estimated that its impact would have been 10 000 times greater than all of today's nuclear weapons combined.

CAMBRIAN

ORDOVICIAN

SILURIAN

DEVONIAN

CARBONIFEROUS

MILLION YEARS AGO (MYA)

505 MYA

438 MYA

408 MYA

360 MYA

END PERMIAN

DURATION	1-5 million years
EXTINCTIONS	More than 90 per cent of all marine species and more than two-thirds of all amphibians and reptiles on land
POSSIBLE CAUSE	Climate change due to glaciation may have been responsible, combined with a massive increase in volcanic activity

SUDDEN DEATH Once common, trilobites died out completely.

END TRIASSIC

DURATION	5 million years
EXTINCTIONS	More than a fifth of all families of marine organisms, as well as a smaller number of groups on land
POSSIBLE CAUSE	Uncertain, although it has been linked to an intense period of volcanic activity

DICYNODONTS These mammal-like reptiles were among the land fatalities.

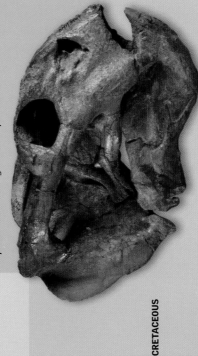

END CRETACEOUS

DURATION	Less than 1 million years
EXTINCTIONS	All dinosaurs and winged reptiles known as pterosaurs. All of the giant marine reptiles apart from the turtles. Many invertebrate animals were also wiped out
POSSIBLE CAUSE	Most authorities are now agreed that a huge meteorite impact caused this mass-extinction event

END OF THE ROAD Like all other dinosaurs, Triceratops disappeared during the mass-extinction event at the end of the Cretaceous period.

PERMIAN

245
MYA

TRIASSIC

208
MYA

JURASSIC

144
MYA

CRETACEOUS

65
MYA

TERTIARY

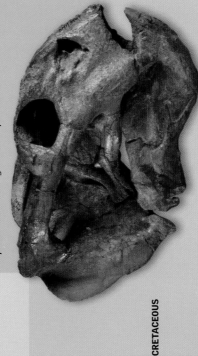

NATURAL DISASTERS

EARTHQUAKES, VOLCANOES, HURRICANES, TSUNAMIS – ALL HAVE A DEVASTATING IMPACT ON THE PLACES WHERE THEY STRIKE. We tend to see these natural disasters in terms of the destruction and havoc they wreak on our own lives, but they also turn the lives of plants and animals upside down.

Violent storms kill many animals, although most are able to escape danger by seeking shelter as winds start to build. Plants must face the worst that the weather has to offer. Hurricanes and typhoons fell many trees and leave others badly damaged. Some plants have evolved mechanisms to cope with the high winds that these violent storms bring. On the Mascarene Islands, east of Madagascar, is a species known as the hurricane palm. It is sadly rare in the wild, not because of storm damage but because of habitat degradation by human activity and browsing of seedlings by introduced animals, including goats.

The species has been saved, however, by cultivation and is extremely popular in tropical and subtropical regions prone to storms. The hurricane palm survives powerful winds by offering them the least possible amount of resistance. Its long, frond-like leaves are extremely tough but flexible at the base, where they meet the trunk. In high winds they blow backwards, moving with the air rather like some

BLOWN FLAT The trunks of spruce trees lie piled like matchsticks after a storm that swept through the Czech Republic in 2007. It will take decades for the forest to recover from such extensive damage.

UNSTOPPABLE FORCE A lava flow creeps across the island of Hawaii, destroying everything in its path.

water weeds do in the currents of rivers. The top half of the trunk is also quite flexible, bending in strong gusts rather than snapping off.

Other palms survive hurricanes in different ways. The royal palm, which is native to southern Florida and the Caribbean, allows its leaves to break away in the strongest winds. Following hurricanes, whole groves of these plants may be devoid of foliage. Although they may look dead they are quick to re-sprout and are soon topped again with a lush canopy of leaves.

It is not just tropical palms that gain protection from storms by shedding their leaves: deciduous trees in temperate climates do, too. Although these trees shed their leaves primarily to conserve energy through the winter, their naked branches are far less prone to being caught in the wind. Winter is usually the time of year when the worst storms batter most temperate countries. Whether by accident or evolutionary design, it is also the time when most trees are best able to cope with them.

Unpredictable forces

Unlike storms, volcanoes and earthquakes are irregular and completely unpredictable. Fortunately, they are also relatively rare, but this combination of factors means that no living things have evolved that can cope with them. Some organisms can tolerate the very high temperatures and unusual chemical conditions around volcanic vents, but none can survive the eruptions themselves. Considering the massive power and heat generated by a volcanic eruption it seems unlikely that any life form could evolve to live through it, even if such events were as frequent and regular as storms.

Volcanoes and earthquakes have the same root cause – the movement of tectonic plates in the Earth's crust and the bubbling up of molten rock beneath them. Earthquakes occur where the edges of plates collide, with one being pushed beneath the other, or where they attempt to slide past one another. These movements are not smooth but occur every so often in judders,

THE LITTLE ICE AGE
In 1600, the Huaynaputina volcano (below) in southern Peru erupted with catastrophic results. It was the biggest eruption anywhere on Earth for 1000 years and its effects were felt the world over and lasted for several decades. The period that followed it has since become known as the Little Ice Age. Ash from Huaynaputina was lifted high into the atmosphere and spread around the globe. Its effects were recorded in England in 1601: 'the month of June was very colde, frosts every morning' wrote one chronicler at the time. In Italy, frozen nights extended into July and the sky was 'overcast' for months. Recent evidence from tree-ring data has shown that the summer of 1601 was by far the coldest in Europe in the past 600 years. Although each subsequent summer improved very slightly, the effects of Huaynaputina was felt in Europe for years after the explosion.

which we experience as earthquakes. Huge frictional forces build up in the rocks and when they are released the land above them shakes, sometimes causing terrible devastation.

Volcanoes that occur where plates collide are caused by the build-up of new molten rock beneath the crust. As one plate is pushed beneath the other, it melts. Most of this molten rock stays beneath the surface, but in places it breaks through and erupts, pumping out molten lava, deadly fumes and huge clouds of ash. Volcanoes also occur in the middle of crustal plates, over points known as hot spots – bulges of molten rock that occur in the mantle. The ash from volcanoes can affect life far from where an eruption takes place. Locally, it often blocks out the Sun. The worst volcanoes can have a global effect on the climate.

The awesome power of the sea

Earthquakes beneath the sea are the main cause of tsunamis. Sometimes the effects can go unnoticed, at other times they leave a trail of utter destruction. The 2004 Asian tsunami was one of the worst natural disasters of recent times, killing more than a quarter of a million people and devastating vast areas of coastline in several countries. Large areas of land were inundated by seawater, which soaked into the ground, killing grasses and other plant life. This in turn left these places unable to support the animal life they had before. Most of the land that was inundated by the tsunami has begun to recover, but it will take years for it to return to its previous state.

The devastation on land was almost matched by that beneath the water, particularly in areas close to shore. Many fringing reefs suffered extensive damage, with coral heads snapped off and scattered by the force of the waves. Fish and other creatures from the reefs were swept inland and left stranded as the water retreated, leaving the coral that remained intact much more sparsely populated than it had been before.

Other problems were caused as the surging water, now carrying a load of churned-up sediment, returned to the sea. Tonnes of mud were dumped on top of many reefs, leaving them buried and cut off from the sunlight that most corals need to survive. Nearer the earthquake's epicentre, the effects on coral reefs were even more extreme. Here, where the Earth's crust itself had moved, many reefs were lifted above the ocean's surface and left high and dry. Others were pulled into deeper water, where some corals found themselves without enough light to survive.

Although the Asian tsunami caused great destruction to large areas of the coastal marine environment, most of these places, like those on land, have since begun to mend themselves. Natural disasters are a part of the way the planet functions and life is incredibly resilient. In time, even the worst wounds inflicted on the Earth disappear.

CHAOS THEORY

IN NATURE, EVEN THE MOST SEEMINGLY INSIGNIFICANT EVENT CAN SNOWBALL INTO SOMETHING VAST. Minute influences can bring about large changes in systems such as the weather, making these systems extremely difficult, even impossible, to predict. The way such systems behave can appear random and chaotic, but in fact there is order underlying all of them. Chaos theory is a mathematical approach that attempts to discover this order so as to understand the forces that bring about change.

In 1960, a meteorologist named Edward Lorenz set up a computer with 12 equations to model the weather. It was not intended to predict the weather, but to produce general schemes of how weather systems might develop. In 1961, Lorenz wanted to replicate part of one sequence again. Rather than starting at the beginning of the sequence, he began in the middle to save time. When he looked at the results, he was amazed to see that the sequence had developed in a completely different direction from the first time. This was totally unexpected. Lorenz realised that he had typed in the figures he had obtained the first time to just three decimal places rather than six. He had typed in the number 0.506, whereas in the original print-out it had read 0.506127. Although the alteration was miniscule, it changed the outcome of the sequence completely.

Lorenz had stumbled across the phenomenon known as sensitive dependence on initial conditions, or the butterfly effect.

He used the idea of a butterfly flapping its wings to explain it. Theoretically, a butterfly flapping its wings might create tiny changes in the atmosphere in one place that ultimately cause a tornado in another place. The flapping wings represent a minute change in initial conditions that can have a huge impact on the way a system develops.

Since Lorenz made his discovery the mathematics used to analyse 'chaotic' systems has become more refined and the processing power offered by computers is much greater. Even so, only the simplest systems susceptible to change in their initial conditions can be accurately predicted. Such systems are usually artificial: a waterwheel, for example, normally turns in the direction of the water flowing over it, but if the rate of flow increases, there comes a point when the wheel starts to turn the opposite way. With enough data on how the volume of water passing over the waterwheel affects its speed, the point at which it will change direction can be worked out.

More complex systems with numerous variables (the waterwheel had just one: the volume of water passing over the wheel per second) are much more difficult to predict. Natural systems, such as the weather, are affected by an almost infinite number of variables and cannot be accurately predicted at all.

SMALL BEGINNINGS With each movement of its wings, a monarch butterfly displaces a tiny amount of air. This action might seem insignificant, but according to chaos theory it has the potential to trigger much bigger events.

LIFE GOES ON

LIFE IS INCREDIBLY RESILIENT. While natural disasters such as a volcanic eruption may wipe out all living things in its path, life quickly returns to recolonise areas from which life was lost.

Even the most apocalyptic disasters are overcome. Nowadays, people talk about saving the planet. While this is usually said with the best intentions, it paints a false picture of the situation. Even in the worst-case scenarios, such as massive climate change or total nuclear war, the planet would survive and so would life. We, on the other hand, might disappear. When people talk about saving the planet, they are really talking about saving the human race and the other more delicate life forms on Earth.

Nature's survivors

Some organisms are naturally tougher than others. Bacteria and many other single-celled organisms seem able to withstand almost anything, occurring on virtually every available surface, including our own skin. Being microscopic in size, they can travel through the air on particles of dust. They are usually the first life forms to begin recolonising an area after a natural disaster, often arriving seconds after the event has taken place.

Multicellular creatures tend to be less resilient. That said, some species have survived several mass-extinction events and are likely candidates to survive any in the future. Scorpions have been on Earth for more than 400 million years, and were among the first creatures to walk on land. That they have existed virtually unchanged for so long should be proof enough of their resilience. Studies have shown that they can tolerate both freezing temperatures and extreme heat.

Another great survivor is the humble woodlouse. Fossils of woodlice date back 50 million years, but it is thought that they have been on Earth much longer – probably at least 160 million years. Woodlice have an incredible tolerance for substances most other creatures find deadly toxic. They can withstand an accumulation of large amounts of lead in their body tissue, for instance, without showing ill effects. Even more remarkable is their tolerance of radiation. Doses of radiation that would kill other animals are shrugged off by woodlice, who carry on with no noticeable problems at all. Even their ability to reproduce is unaffected. A post-Armageddon nuclear winter for humans could be a summer of opportunity for woodlice.

Among vertebrates, perhaps the greatest survivors are sharks. Like woodlice, sharks can tolerate high levels of toxins. Rather than spreading through a shark's body tissue, chemicals become concentrated

BORN SURVIVOR Scorpions have survived a succession of extinction events unchanged.

in the cartilaginous tissue that makes up the creature's skeleton and fins. Sharks' fins have been found to contain extremely high levels of mercury, the combined result of sharks being at the top of the food chain (where toxins are always most concentrated) and the increasing pollution in the seas. Far from being beneficial to health, as traditionally believed among Chinese communities, sharkfin soup is becoming an ever-greater health risk. The sharks themselves suffer no ill effects from the high levels of mercury and other toxins they carry: by concentrating them in their cartilage they essentially lock them away.

Sharks have lived through all of the known major extinction events since vertebrates first appeared. They are perhaps better equipped than any others to survive similar events in the future. Other groups of animals will surely disappear completely, just as happened in the past. Life itself, however, will go on.

Bouncing back

The cataclysmic events that trigger mass extinctions are the greatest challenges that life forms are ever likely to face. Natural disasters such as volcanoes, fires and tsunamis are devastating on a local scale, but rarely threaten entire species. In the immediate aftermath of a natural disaster, large areas of land are often left barren, but life is usually quick to return. Often within days, the land starts to heal and the ground becomes covered with new growth as plants re-sprout and seeds buried beneath the ash burst into life.

Volcanic ash beds, like those left by wild fires, are soon recolonised by plants. Surviving plants may simply grow up through the ash. Others sprout from seeds cast in bird droppings or blown in by the wind. As every gardener knows, plants with wind-borne seeds are specialists at colonising freshly exposed patches of soil, and volcanic ash beds offer similar conditions for these seeds to take hold in. Ironically, considering the violence and destruction that takes place when it is created, volcanic ash forms the basis for some of the richest soil beds on the planet. It is for this reason that so many farmers risk living on the flanks of volcanic mountains, even ones that are far from extinct.

Lava flows burn and bury everything in their paths, coating the land with a new skin of rock, and often remain barren for years. Even here, though, living organisms can get a toe-hold. Slowly but surely, life moves in to reclaim the land. The first living things to colonise lava beds, apart from microorganisms, are usually lichens. Lichens form from symbiotic partnerships between single-celled algae and fungi, and they produce energy by photosynthesis. The fungus forms the body of the lichen and removes minerals from whatever it is growing on, including rock. Some of these are passed to the algal cells, which provide the fungus with food through photosynthesis.

Each lichen, although technically consisting of two separate living organisms, behaves as one. The symbiotic partnership is so close that in most cases neither fungus nor alga is able to survive on its own. Lichens are extremely slow growing, but because they can live on bare rock they are found in many places where other multicellular organisms could not survive. As

LIFE AFTER DEATH A conifer sapling grows among the ash and rubble thrown out by the explosion of Mount St Helen's in 1980.

well as being able to live without soil, they can tolerate high winds and extremely low temperatures, and are often the only visible organisms living on mountaintops.

Lichens rarely have beds of cooled lava to themselves for long. Seeds blown into cracks in the rock settle on volcanic ash and take root. As they grow into plants, shed leaves and die, their remains add organic matter, and so the cracks slowly accumulate layers of soil. Given enough time, lava beds can disappear beneath layers of organic matter. Yellowstone National Park is a perfect example. Two million years ago the whole area was a wasteland of lava and ash, following the eruption of North America's most violent supervolcano. Today, it is a rich natural habitat full of life, a showpiece of wilderness in one of the world's most populous and developed countries.

A matter of chance

After natural disasters, such as earthquakes, species return. After cataclysmic extinction events, survival can be a matter of chance and life can take a new direction. Tortoises and turtles have been on the Earth for 215 million years and were among the reptiles that survived the extinction event at the end of the Cretaceous period that wiped out the dinosaurs some 65 million

years ago. Nobody is certain why tortoises and turtles survived, but it may have been due to their slow metabolism, which would have enabled them to survive for long periods without food.

Another group that survived were the early mammals. The ancestors of the three major modern mammal groups – monotremes, marsupials and placental mammals – had all emerged by 110 million years ago. By the end of the Cretaceous there were 15 known mammal families spread across these groups. These creatures were all small, insectivorous and nocturnal. When the dinosaurs disappeared, they were able to emerge into the open and take over newly vacated niches. By the early Eocene epoch, around 15 million years later, 78 mammal families existed. Over the following millennia, as continents shifted and collided and the global climate changed, mammals spread and diversified to become the dominant group on the planet.

ANCIENT SURVIVOR A giant tortoise on the Alcedo volcano, on the Galápagos island of Isabela. Researchers believe that the tortoise population was severely reduced when the volcano erupted 100 000 years ago, leaving a small group with possibly only one female. Yet the Alcedo population survived and is now the largest in the Galápagos.

FACTS

MASS EXTINCTIONS HAPPEN EVERY 26-28 MILLION YEARS on average as part of the evolutionary cycle, according to scientists. Following these events new species evolve to replace lost ones and add to the survivors.

BEETLES WERE AMONG THE FIRST LIVING things to appear on Mount St Helen's after the eruption of 1980, attracted by the remains of millions of tiny spiders that rained down on the slopes of the volcano.

4554 SPECIES of mammals are known to exist in the world today.

FACTS

THE HUM
ELEMENT

AN 7

THE EARTH TODAY LOOKS QUITE UNLIKE IT EVER DID BEFORE. Throughout the planet's history, natural geological, climatic and even extraterrestrial events have wrought great, sometimes cataclysmic, changes. Now, after billions of years of manipulation by natural forces, the human element has begun to affect the face of the Earth. Today, where forests have gone, it is because we have cut them down; where glaciers melt, it is because of the fuels we burn. We have transformed the natural landscape through agriculture and covered ever-increasing areas with roads and houses (left). Our power as a single species is unprecedented in the history of life on the planet. How we wield that power will affect our own future, for we are part of the natural world, entirely dependent on the Earth and other living things to survive.

HUNTING AND FISHING

TODAY'S CATCH Tuna fish lined up in a market in Tokyo. The flesh of these fish will be used for sushi and tuna steaks, but countless more like them are processed and canned on factory ships for sale in supermarkets around the world. Most species of tuna are now threatened due to overfishing.

HUMANS HAVE ALWAYS BEEN HUNTERS. We evolved to eat meat, and there are physical clues to remind us of the fact – the appendix, for example. In herbivores, this is a large and daily-used part of the gut, a sac containing the bacteria needed to digest plant food. After countless millennia of disuse, the human appendix has all but disappeared and can be removed without any ill effect to the functioning of the body.

Before the advent of farming around 12 000 years ago, all human beings lived as hunter-gatherers – in some parts of the world they still do. And for thousands of years after that, human hunting had very little impact on the other species with which we share our planet. While humans were still relatively few in number, the numbers of animals they killed were relatively few. But as populations grew and people spread, that changed. In some cases, human beings hunted entire species to extinction. In New Zealand, for example, a whole family of giant birds – the moas – had disappeared by the 16th century. Flightless relatives of Australia's cassowaries and emu, they were the biggest birds on the planet – the largest, the giant moa, stood 3 m tall and weighed up to 250 kg. New Zealand's Maori people are thought to have arrived on the islands between AD 800 and 1300, having travelled from Polynesia in the central Pacific. By around 1550, they had wiped out all nine species of moas that had thrived there. Being flightless, and with no experience of predators, moas were easy prey, and a single kill provided large quantities of meat.

There are parallel tales all over the globe. Not long after the last moa disappeared, the auroch died out in Europe. The ancestors of today's domesticated cattle, aurochs once ranged across Europe, including Britain. The last of these huge beasts, which stood 1.75 m tall at the shoulder, died in Poland in 1627.

Present danger

Hunting remains a threat to the survival of many land animals, even though hunting for subsistence is increasingly rare. In Africa, more and more people are living in towns and cities, but they have not lost their appetite for wild animal meat. The majority of wild animals killed in Africa today, including gorillas

and chimpanzees, die at the hands of hunters to be sold in markets as 'bush meat'. Africa is far from alone in this. In China, people eat wild animal meat on a major scale, and various body parts of wild animals are also used in traditional Chinese medicine – rhinoceros horn, among many others. The merits of traditional Chinese remedies are debatable, but hundreds of millions of people trust and rely on them, and the demand for ingredients fuels hunting in many parts of the world, including the poaching of rhinos and other endangered species, such as tigers.

Many Western countries rely heavily on wild animals for food, although this fact often goes unrecognised, since the animals come from the oceans. Fishing is a multibillion dollar industry that provides jobs and sustains coastal communities. It is also the biggest single threat to life in the sea. The term 'overfishing' did not exist until the 20th century, but it is now familiar to most people. When it comes to fish stocks, out of sight really is out of mind: often a problem is not noticed until seabirds and other creatures reliant on fish start to decline. For as long as there are people, hunting and fishing will continue. The challenge is how to make these practices sustainable, for the sake of the environment, of the survival of other species and of the people who depend on them for food or their livelihoods.

HUNTING FOR DINNER The San people (Bushmen) of Namibia still use bows and arrows to hunt game, just as their ancestors – and ours – did for centuries before them. Small-scale hunting like this holds little threat for the environment.

DOMESTICATION

TODAY, DOMESTICATED STOCK, SUCH AS CATTLE, SHEEP AND PIGS, VASTLY OUTNUMBER LARGE WILD MAMMALS. Looked at from a purely biological perspective, these farmed mammals can be considered among the world's dominant animal species. They are far more widespread and numerous than they would have been if they had never been domesticated but left in the wild.

According to archaeological evidence, humans started domesticating stock animals around 10 000 years ago, beginning with goats in what is now the Middle East. Other creatures besides large mammals also benefited from the process. The chicken, for instance, is descended from the red junglefowl, a member of the pheasant family, which still lives wild in the forests of southern Asia. Cats and dogs have also been winners, going with us to all corners of the globe. In many places, they have returned to the

WORLD TRAVELLERS Chickens scrabble for food in a village in Bolivia. From their origins as junglefowl in southern Asia, chickens have spread around the globe, all due to their domestication by humans.

wild. The dingo, for example, arrived in Australia with the country's early human settlers. It had been domesticated by then but was little changed from the wolf, the ancestor it shares with all domestic dogs.

Man's oldest friend

Archaeological finds suggest that dogs, rather than stock animals, were the first animals to be domesticated – probably 10–15 000 years ago. Today, they are massively changed in relation to their wild ancestors, with 195 recognised breeds, each with its own characteristics. Dog diversity is the result of

GENETIC ENGINEERING

Genetic engineering is the next logical scientific step after selective breeding. When animals reproduce, all of the parents' genetic material combines in their offspring. In genetic engineering, the specific gene combinations that cause particular physical characteristics are extracted from the DNA of the cell of one individual and spliced into that of another. This technique permits the detailed combination of specific genetic material within a single species, and also the possibility of DNA from one species being added to the genetic make-up of another.

selective breeding. Rather than choosing, and perhaps fighting for, their own partners, dogs have had mates imposed upon them by humans, who wished them to pass on certain characteristics to their puppies.

In dogs bred for hunting, speed and strength were usually the main traits selected. In working animals, such as sheepdogs, intelligence and obedience were more important. Many of the newer breeds have been bred simply for the way they look – their size and colour, the length of their fur, even the droop of their ears or skin. Yet even though they display a greater variety in appearance than any other animal, domesticated or wild, all dogs, from the Chihuahua to the Great Dane, belong to the same species (*Canis familiaris*) and are able to interbreed with one another and with wolves.

One look at the results of selective breeding shows that it is a powerful force for change. In farm animals kept for food, the traits selected for have included meat or milk yield, or the number of eggs laid. Sheep have been selectively bred for their wool in some parts of the world, for their meat or milk in others. In recent decades, the whole process has quickened, helped in part by the development and implementation of new techniques, such as artificial insemination. The latest weapon in the breeders' arsenal – and also the most controversial – is genetic engineering (see box, above).

All animals that have undergone selective breeding look significantly different from their ancestors. Domestic cattle are descended from the massive auroch (see page 133), while the mouflon, a 1.2 m tall mountain grazer with extravagantly

curved horns, probably gave rise to domestic sheep. Most domesticated animals also tend to be much more docile than their forerunners.

Gone to seed

Most of the world lives on a staple diet of grass seeds – rice, wheat, oats and barley are all varieties of grasses that have been domesticated and selectively bred. Besides being eaten cooked as whole grains, they are ground into flour, which is then used to make bread, cakes and other products. Like domesticated animals, these grasses differ greatly from their ancestors. They have been selectively bred primarily for their yield of grain, but also for resistance to pests. Now they are among the most widespread and successful plants on the planet, covering vast areas of land almost to the exclusion of everything else.

NEW ZEALAND LAMB In 1982, at the height of sheep farming in New Zealand, there were more than 70 million sheep in the country, compared with a human population of fewer than 4 million.

TAMING THE LAND

HUMANS HAVE ALTERED VAST AREAS OF ONCE WILD LAND TO SERVE THEIR NEEDS. Agriculture, in particular, has swallowed huge swathes of wilderness, and perhaps more than anything else, it has been the key to the success of our species. Before agriculture existed, everybody was a hunter-gatherer, and few people were able to live in any one place for long. In most parts of the world, people had to keep moving in order to find enough food and not exhaust the resources of an area. Agriculture allowed people to settle in permanent homes, enabling conurbations to form. Even now, the greatest cities would quickly die without it.

No going back

Agriculture also helped people to spread to new parts of the planet. Migrants took domesticated plants and animals with them and so ensured themselves a source of food. Even in places that we might consider completely wild, evidence of this practice exists. The rainforests of Papua New Guinea are today home to wild pigs, which are not native to the region but were brought there by early settlers. By using the land to

SEA OF GRASS Wheat is a grass that was first domesticated in western Asia. Selectively bred and tended by humans, it has become one of the most successful and widespread plants on Earth, with a dramatic impact on landscapes worldwide, as here on the Great Plains of the USA.

produce food, rather than simply harvesting what was naturally there, we have been able to support an ever-growing population. Today, there are some 6.5 billion people on Earth – more than twice as many as there were in 1960. Without agriculture, that population explosion could not have been sustained.

In our modern world, agriculture is an absolute and undeniable necessity. Farmland surrounds our cities and in the developed world covers most of the space in between. The great arable ranches of North America are a spectacular example – seemingly endless plains of wheat and corn, without hedgerows or fences, divided only by the occasional road. To maximise crop yields, these farms are virtually devoid of natural vegetation. The crop is king, and herbicides and insecticides ensure that nothing hampers its growth.

Man-made landscapes

Elsewhere, the landscape may be more pleasing to the eye, but its function is no less practical. The terraced paddy fields of Bali, for instance, are entirely man-made; the level 'steps' cut in the hillsides permit rice to be grown on what would otherwise be sloping ground. Unlike most grasses, rice requires a huge amount of water at certain stages to grow well, so paddy fields need to be regularly flooded. The Balinese terraces are walled with mud at the edges to hold the water in and joined by intricate systems of ditches and tiny waterfalls to ensure proper irrigation. Bali's terraced paddy fields are part of the character

of the island's landscape and attract tourists from all over the world, but their purpose is strictly workaday. Rice is the staple diet for more than half of the world's population, feeding 2 billion people in India and China alone.

In Britain, too, agriculture defines much of the landscape. Like the rice terraces of Bali, the patchwork of fields that makes up the English countryside is entirely artificial, the result of centuries of farming and the periodic division and redivision of land into parcels. Hedgerows started out as boundaries defining ownership while at the same time stopping livestock from straying. Yet, they have become so closely associated with the landscape that their destruction in the 1970s was considered by many to be little short of vandalism. The value of hedgerows as havens and highways for wildlife has since been recognised, and a system of grants and controls has been put in place to safeguard and replace them. According to government figures, between 1990 and 1993, more than 10 000 km of hedgerows were planted or restored each year.

Despite such measures, the constant spread of farming places pristine territory in danger. Worldwide, the natural habitat most threatened by agriculture is grassland, which lends itself so easily to farming that in most places it has already been swallowed up. Since the invention of the plough, huge areas of grassland have been turned over and replanted with species useful to us. Where the ground has been too stony or poor for crops, we have used it for grazing livestock, a process

AROUND 75 PER CENT OF UK LAND IS USED FOR FARMING.
By contrast, census figures show that in the much larger United States, only 41.4 per cent of land is given over to agriculture, of which 46.3 per cent is under crops and 42.1 per cent used for pasture. Most of the remaining farmland is made up of woodland.

23 PER CENT LESS pesticide is used on UK farms than ten years ago, according to the Farming & Wildlife Advisory Group.

RICE HAS BEEN GROWN FOR 10 000 YEARS.
Some 140 000 cultivated varieties are known.

FACTS

ALTERED LANDSCAPE Palm trees and banana plants grow among the paddy fields in a valley in Bali. The landscape is stunningly beautiful, and to a very large extent is man-made.

that also greatly alters the make-up of the plant life within the soil and that can lead to plant extinctions. It is less efficient than crop-growing in terms of yield from the land it uses: much more crop-based food can be produced per hectare than meat. This is because plants sit at the bottom of the food chain and grazing animals on the next rung up. The latter consume plants in order to generate meat, but in the process a lot of the energy from those plants is used up and lost.

In Central and South America large areas of rainforest have been cleared to raise cattle for beef, mostly bought by other countries. Tropical farmers have an advantage over their counterparts in temperate climates in that their cattle can feed on grass all year round and have no need of hay, silage (fermented plant matter) or other winter food. This, combined with much lower labour costs, makes Latin American beef much cheaper than beef produced elsewhere. With the global market for beef growing, along with the demand for cheaper food, the outcome seems inevitable: more forest will be lost to pasture.

The challenge ahead

With land in demand to support ever increasing numbers of people, true wilderness will become more and more scarce. The challenge is to manage it, earmarking the most important and diverse wilderness areas for preservation and ensuring that what is lost to agriculture is used in the most productive way. Although not wild, farmland can also be home to wildlife, and, like the Balinese paddy fields, may have charm and beauty in its own right, which makes it worth conserving.

ORIGINS OF AGRICULTURE

Archaeological research shows that farming began around 12 000 years ago towards the end of the last Ice Age. While northern Europe was a frozen waste, people in what is now Egypt were growing crops. In Egypt, as everywhere, the climate was colder than it is today, but still warm enough for plants to grow. The earliest crops were types of barley and wheat, domesticated forms of grasses that grew wild locally. Shortly afterwards, barley-growing began in Mesopotamia, a region that today includes Iraq.

For 2000 years, farming was just arable, although enough food was produced for villages to grow into towns. Then, some 10 000 years ago, people began keeping animals for their milk and meat. Goats descended from the bezoar ibex – a mountain goat from south-west Asia – were the first 'farm animals', followed by sheep (see page 135). At this stage, animals were not penned but kept by herders, who travelled with them in a continual search for grazing.

URBANISATION

A QUICK GLANCE AT A CITY MAP CAN OFTEN GIVE AN IDEA OF THE LANDSCAPE BEFORE THE CONURBATION SPREAD, PARTICULARLY IN THE NAMES OF STREETS AND DISTRICTS. Forest Hill in south London, for instance, was once a wooded hilly area; today, it is covered with suburban housing.

Elsewhere in London, St John's Wood was originally just that before becoming absorbed into the capital, while even Smithfield and Spitalfields, on the fringes of the City of London, carry echoes of a rural past in their names.

Concrete jungles

Towns and cities cover only a tiny fraction of the Earth's land area, yet where they do occur they transform the landscape completely. The biggest change urbanisation makes is that it covers the ground with concrete, bricks and tarmac so that huge areas of soil simply disappear. For human convenience, this is exactly what is required, but such a landscape is largely inhospitable to wildlife. Like farmland, towns and cities are managed environments. Life pushed out of urbanised areas has a tough time getting back in, at least as long as these areas remain inhabited by humans.

CITY DWELLER The red fox has become a common sight in Britain's towns and cities, taking advantage of the food people throw away.

Where buildings and streets are well maintained, plants and animals are usually uprooted, driven out or exterminated if they get a toehold.

Even so, some species have made cities their home and thrive there. Most of them are adaptable, or flexible in their habits, and live off food that we inadvertently provide. The best-known and most notorious are rodents such as the brown rat and the house mouse, which do so well in cities that they are usually much more common there than in the countryside. Both often live in buildings, and as its name suggests, the house mouse is particularly invasive, finding its way in through the smallest of gaps. Once inside a building, it makes its home in a secure nook or cranny, often behind skirting boards or beneath the floor. The house mouse, like the brown rat, is usually active at night, emerging to feed when the city's human residents are tucked up in bed.

Other city-dwelling creatures may be more endearing, although they, too, can cause a nuisance. In North America, raccoons have adapted well to urban life, eating discarded food, scavenging from dustbins and making dens in chimneys, cellars, attics and under outside decking. These urban 'masked bandits' tend to live more densely than their rural counterparts. In Ontario, Canada, for example, the average rural population density is estimated at 4–12 raccoons per km^2, while in an urban setting this figure rises to 8–18, and an extreme figure of 100 animals per km^2 has been recorded.

URBAN SPRAWL Even in densely populated urban areas, such as Guatemala City (below) in Central America, green spaces survive, providing a home for a variety of wild animals.

Britain has its equivalent in the urban fox, which also finds much of its food among human leftovers. Like city-dwelling raccoons, urban foxes tend to live in more dense populations than rural ones, reflecting the comparative ease with which they can find food in the city. According to 2004 estimates, Britain has an urban fox population of around 33 000 – of which perhaps 10 000 live inside the M25 – while 225 000 live in the countryside, a much larger area.

Contrary to popular belief, city foxes are not incomers from the countryside but are born and bred 'townies', having first infiltrated urban areas on a large scale with the construction of many suburban housing estates in the 1930s. In the suburbs, an adult fox's territory may cover 80–120 gardens. While country foxes have dens underground, the favourite haunt of the urban fox is beneath the garden shed: an estimated 75 per cent of London's fox cubs are born in such surroundings.

Life on tall buildings

Among other animals that thrive in urban surroundings, perhaps none is more familiar than the feral pigeon. Descended from the rock dove *(Columba livia)*, a bird of the cliffs, the pigeon may have been domesticated as much as 10 000 years ago, initially for food. People have since given rise to some 200 varieties of this bird, by means of selective breeding for looks, speed or homing ability. Over the centuries, many individual pigeons escaped or were released back to the wild, thus becoming feral, or semi-wild. They found cities to their liking, surviving on a diet of scraps, and nesting on the ledges of buildings – satisfactory substitutes for cliffs.

Less visible than the pigeon, and less commonly associated with city settings is the peregrine falcon *(Falco peregrinus)*, but it has also settled successfully in urban environments. A cliff-dwelling bird like the pigeon, this crow-sized raptor is known to

nest on a range of buildings, including cathedrals and power station cooling towers. In France, 16 pairs of peregrines were reported to have raised a total of 25 young in urban settings – from Strasbourg in the north to Albi in the south – in 2006.

The move to the city

In recent decades, there has been a huge worldwide migration of people from the countryside into urban areas, particularly in developing countries. According to the United Nations Population Fund (UNFPA), from 2008, for the first time in history, more people worldwide will live in towns and cities than in rural areas. The driving force behind this shift is poverty and increased population densities in the countryside. With the same amount of land being pushed to support ever more people, many have migrated to cities in search of a living. In the developing world, few of these new city-dwellers have found

a better life. Indeed, far from improving, the situation of the majority has worsened, and most of these migrants live in vast shanty towns huddled around the older, more established city centres. With large numbers of people crowded together in unsanitary conditions, many shanty towns have become breeding grounds for disease.

The effects of urbanisation go far beyond the world's conurbations themselves. Towns and cities require regular supplies of food and other goods just in order to exist, and these rarely come from the immediate vicinity. People, too, move in and out of urban areas on a regular basis. As towns and cities have grown, so have the various transport networks that link them all together.

The modern world is criss-crossed with roads and railways; they can even be found running through otherwise untouched wilderness. Since railway lines are silent and empty for most of the time, except near the edges of the largest cities, they have relatively little impact on the natural world. The same cannot be said for roads. As traffic has increased, roads have become a major

LANDSCAPE TRANSFORMED Before and after pictures of the 43 hectare London Wetland Centre. A wasteland on the banks of the Thames has been transformed into a haven for wildlife, including migrating birds.

LIGHTS OVER THE WORLD

A composite satellite image shows the world at night. This is when the human imprint on the planet is perhaps easiest to see, as lights from roads, towns and cities shine out into space, showing their exact positions on the globe. Artificial light is a good indicator of population density, particularly in the developed world, where street and road lights are common.

The darkest areas show forests, where few people live. Grasslands, deserts and areas covered by snow and ice appear a lighter purplish blue.

Although city lights are important for safety, they require huge amounts of energy to keep them going. Another side effect is that they colour the sky, making it harder to see stars at night in the urban areas they illuminate.

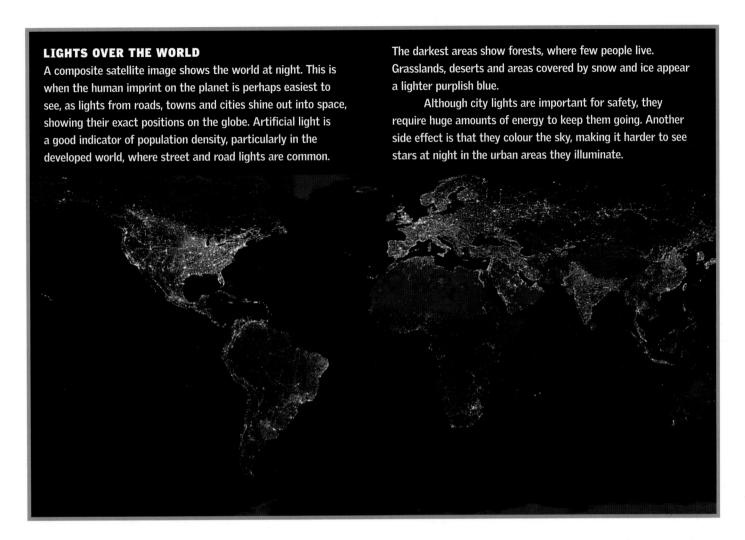

hazard for wildlife. In some places almost as many animals are killed on the roads as die from natural causes. For creatures near the top of the food chain, such as foxes, which have few natural predators, being killed on a road is often the most common cause of death. As well as killing animals, busy roads create terrifying barriers that keep populations of animals apart. Where small groups of a species become isolated, inbreeding can occur, weakening the group's genetic make-up, with the result that future generations will be less able to combat disease.

The cost of buying

Urbanisation goes hand in hand with industrialisation. In Europe and the United States, the major growth of towns and cities took place in the 18th and 19th centuries during the Industrial Revolution, as rural workers flocked to urban areas in search of jobs.

Elsewhere, urbanisation is a continuing process, which still creates jobs and wealth – but not without cost. Industries such as construction and manufacturing use huge quantities of natural materials, including fossil fuels.

Reports published by BP and German academics suggest that shipping, which carries 90 per cent of the world's freight, is responsible for 5 per cent of all emissions of carbon dioxide, the gas that contributes most to global warming.

In recent years, China has expanded industrially on a grand scale, with particular focus on manufacturing. This growth has led to China overtaking the USA as the world's biggest emitter of greenhouse gases. While urbanisation and development within the country itself are partly responsible, multinational companies from the West have also been a major factor as they move manufacturing bases to China. A large proportion of the country's greenhouse gas emissions is created producing goods to be sold in North America and Europe.

Further environmental costs are incurred in getting these and other goods to market. The damage done by aircraft is much discussed: during taxiing, take-off and landing for a single journey, a jumbo jet generates as much polluting nitrogen oxide as an average car does over a total of 85 000 km. The cost to the environment of sending freight by sea, however, has only recently come to light. Reports published by BP and German academics suggest that shipping, which carries 90 per cent of the world's freight, is responsible for 5 per cent of all emissions of carbon dioxide, the gas that contributes most to global warming.

DIVIDING LINE Farmland hugs the border of the Emas National Park in Brazil. This picture illustrates the problem facing the world's wild forests today. From a business perspective, the land they occupy could often be put to more profitable use, but in ecological terms the loss of forests is disastrous. Most of the plants and animals that live in them are unable to adapt and do not survive in the industrial farmland that often takes the place of the forest, so the biodiversity of the area is lost.

CUTTING DOWN THE FORESTS

TEN THOUSAND YEARS AGO, FOREST COVERED TWO-THIRDS OF THE PLANET. **Today, that figure has halved.** The difference between then and now is down to a single animal species – our own. *Homo sapiens* has altered the planet to its own needs more completely than any other creature before it. In the case of the forests, they have been cut down to make way for agriculture and to provide wood for burning and timber for building.

Deforestation has happened in waves. The first great wave occurred in Europe, once covered with temperate woodland, which disappeared as the human population gradually rose. Even before the spread of the Roman Empire, people had already deforested much of the continent. Most of the forests that still exist today in Europe are degraded or managed woodland. The only untouched pocket of original wild wood straddles the border between Belarus and Poland, its centre protected in the Bialowieza National Park.

As Europe's forests melted away, humans were clearing woodlands in other parts of the world as well. The greatest early clearances followed the spread of agriculture: in China and India, for instance, forests shrank as populations grew and the demand for farmland rose. In these places, however, large areas of forest survived intact until fairly recent times. The next great wave of deforestation followed the spread of Europeans around the globe. As they settled in new places, they cleared woodlands to create farms and for building timber. Again, however, the process was relatively small-scale at first. At the start of the 20th century, many of the world's greatest tracts of forest were still standing.

A growing problem

In the past 100 years, the pace of deforestation has accelerated, and trees are now disappearing at a faster rate than ever before. The areas most at risk are the tropical rainforests, which are being felled both to provide high-quality timber – most of which is exported – and to free up land for farming. In the last decade of the 20th century, South America lost more than 4 per cent of its forest cover, and Africa almost 8 per cent. In the 15 years from 1990 to 2005, Indonesia lost more than 28 million hectares – nearly a quarter of its forest cover. According to the UN's Food and Agriculture Organization, 7.3 million hectares of forest were lost worldwide each year between 2000 and 2005.

Logging in tropical rainforests is big business, making a few people incredibly rich. The timber taken has no shortage of buyers. Much of it is used in construction, an industry which continues to grow along with the number of people on the planet. Most tropical rainforest trees are so-called hardwood species, including mahogany, teak and rosewood, as opposed to softwood conifers, such as spruce, larch and pine. As its name suggests, hardwood timber is incredibly durable. It is also used in the manufacture of furniture, particularly garden furniture and other objects destined for a life outdoors.

As long as people need wood, logging is bound to carry on, but it cannot continue at its current rate unless it is properly managed and controlled. Unlike fossil fuels, trees are renewable, but they have to be planted or allowed to seed naturally to ensure a continuous supply. Every day, areas of tropical rainforest are clear felled – all the trees from that area are removed – as loggers seek short-term gain at the expense of long-term sustainability. The industry does not have to work in this way. Some operators log sustainably, by removing individual trees while leaving the forest around them intact, giving it time to recover and allowing new trees to grow.

SCORCHED EARTH Slash-and-burn farmers plant maize on a hillside in Madagascar where forest stood just weeks before. Unlike industrial farming, slash and burn is mostly carried out by people growing food to survive.

ECO TIMBER

Wood and products made from wood sourced under managed conditions receive the stamp of approval from organisations such as the Forestry Stewardship Council (FSC), with its headquarters in Bonn, Germany, and offices worldwide. This passes the burden of responsibility to consumers. Put simply, products with the FSC mark (below) are environmentally sound. Those without it may use wood from clear felling or illegal logging.

Deforestation and global warming

Forests are the natural home of a huge range of plants and animals, and deforestation has a massive impact on them. Tropical rainforests are particularly rich, supporting more species than any other habitat on the planet. A single hectare of rainforest may have more than 480 different species of tree growing in it – compared with perhaps six dominant species in a similar area of temperate forest. When forests disappear, their inhabitants disappear with them – deforestation is one of the main causes of extinction today.

Forest cover and its loss also have an impact on the atmosphere. Trees produce oxygen and remove carbon dioxide from the air. Uncontrolled logging may well be helping to drive global warming. Another activity – slash-and-burn farming – is definitely a factor in global warming. This is the process by which forest is cut down and set alight to make way for crops. The fires not only clear away trees and other plant growth, they also produce large amounts of carbon dioxide and other greenhouse gases.

Driven by population pressure and the basic human need for food, slash-and-burn farming is gradually eroding the edges of many of the world's tropical forests. Many slash-and-burn farmers are poor people, who grow crops to feed themselves. The problem with this type of farming is that it is not sustainable. Once the forest has been removed, the soil contains only enough nutrients to grow crops for a year or two. When the soil is exhausted, the farmers repeat the process and clear more forest.

As well as being important natural habitats and producing oxygen, forests play other crucial roles. The roots of their trees bind soils together. If they are removed, particularly from hilly areas, soil is soon eroded and sometimes completely washed away. Forests also soak up water, so deforestation can lead to floods. The catastrophic inundations that have affected Bangladesh in recent decades have largely been blamed on deforestation upstream. Severe floods and mudslides elsewhere in the world have also been linked to deforestation.

Even where the process of deforestation is being reversed, as it is in many parts of the world, the results do not always benefit diversity. Where reforestation is undertaken by conservationists, native species are planted. Most new areas of forest, however, are plantations grown for profit, which tend to be of a single species. The trees are destined to be logged for timber or some other economic purposes. Indonesia, for instance, has huge oil palm plantations where once it had rainforest. The oil extracted from the palm fruit is used in the production of a wide range of food and cosmetic products.

TREE FARM Lines of young conifers cover a hill in New Zealand, next to mature trees planted decades before. Plantations produce as much oxygen and consume as much carbon dioxide as natural forests, making them good buffers to global warming, but unless they consist of native trees, they are usually poor habitats for wildlife.

SOME OF THE WORST FOREST FIRES

OF MODERN TIMES STRUCK INDONESIA IN 1997-8. They were the most destructive fires ever suffered by the South-east Asian nation. Most badly hit was the province of East Kalimantan, on the island of Borneo, where 5.2 million hectares – around 25 per cent of the total land area – was affected.

Indonesia has been plagued by conflagrations since 1982-3, when fires destroyed an area of forest in East Kalimantan equal to the size of Belgium. They have been put down to a combination of drought brought on by the ENSO (El Niño-Southern Oscillation) climate event – which disrupts rainfall patterns – and human activity, including slash-and-burn agriculture, plantation clearance and logging operations. Loggers not only clear forests, they also make high-intensity fires more likely by leaving behind combustible debris and waste not found in natural woodlands. Conflagrations occur when clearance fires get out of control.

Besides destroying vast swathes of forest, and with it both wildlife habitat and the wildlife itself, the 1997-8 fires produced a noxious smog that spread over six neighbouring countries, reducing sunlight and affecting animals and people alike. According to some sources, the Malaysian city of Kuching registered 800 on the Pollutant Standards Index – a score of 300 is considered 'hazardous'. The long-term health of some 70 million people was put at risk.

Although rains that arrived in mid-1998 put out most of the fires, by then the intensity had ignited huge areas of peat soils. These are notoriously difficult to extinguish and have since pumped millions of tonnes of greenhouse gases into the atmosphere.

DATE: July 1997 to May 1998

AREA DAMAGED: Around
9.7 million hectares

CARBON DIOXIDE EMISSIONS:
More than 700 million tonnes
(22 per cent of the world's
1997-8 CO_2 production)

ECONOMIC COST: Around
US $9 billion

INDONESIA

FOREST FIRE

VITAL STATS

LETTING UV
BACK IN

BEFORE LIFE BEGAN,
ULTRAVIOLET (UV)
RADIATION FROM
THE SUN BOMBARDED
OUR PLANET. The arrival
of photosynthesising
organisms, such as cyanobacteria, algae and later plants, filled
the atmosphere with oxygen. High in the stratosphere, some of this oxygen
turned gradually into ozone, forming a protective barrier which served to keep most
ultraviolet light out (see page 48). With the ozone layer in place, life was able to move
safely from the seas onto the land.

Breaches in the barrier

In recent decades, the ozone layer has been under threat – the first time this has
happened in the hundreds of millions of years since it formed. Man-made chemicals
have found their way into the stratosphere and begun to break down the ozone layer,
thinning it and eroding the protection it gives to living things. If the ozone layer were
to disappear completely, most life on land would probably disappear along with it. The
only places where life could continue unaffected on land would be in environments
permanently out of direct sunlight, such as gaps beneath rocks. Life in the sea would be
largely unaffected. Water, like ozone, acts as a barrier to ultraviolet radiation, soaking
it up before it can penetrate very far.

The harmful effects of ultraviolet radiation on living tissue are well known. For fair-
skinned people, even an hour in direct sunlight can cause sunburn. Continued damage
to the skin from repeated sunbathing can lead to skin cancer. Both sunburn and skin
cancer are caused by the ultraviolet radiation in sunlight – sunlight that has already

**If the ozone layer were
to disappear completely,
most life on land would
probably disappear along
with it. The only places
where life could continue
unaffected on land would
be in environments
permanently out of
direct sunlight, such as
gaps beneath rocks.**

*PROTECTIVE LAYER Ozone is most common in
the lower stratosphere, where it filters the Sun's
ultraviolet light, blocking the shorter wavelengths
that are most harmful to life on Earth.*

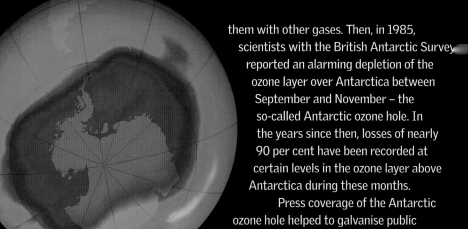

ANTARCTIC GAP The ozone hole over Antarctica is not totally devoid of ozone, but is an area where its concentration has greatly diminished. This picture shows the hole as it was in 2006.

passed through the ozone layer. Without the ozone layer in place, the amount of ultraviolet radiation striking the Earth and its inhabitants would be multiplied many times over. Even the toughest plants and animals would find it hard to survive for long.

How ozone decays

The thickness of the ozone layer varies and always has done even under natural conditions. It is generally thickest over the poles and thinnest over the Equator. It also varies with the seasons – it is usually thinner in the Northern Hemisphere in autumn and thicker in the spring. These natural fluctuations are a result of various factors, including the circulation of the atmosphere.

The new threat to the ozone layer comes from negatively charged atoms, or ions, of chlorine and fluorine, which break away from chemical compounds known as chlorofluorocarbons (CFCs) under the influence of ultraviolet light. For a long time, CFCs were widely used throughout the world as a propellant in aerosol sprays. They were also employed in a variety of other applications, including refrigerators and air conditioning units, for creating foam and for cleaning electronics components.

At ground level CFCs are stable, but when they reach the stratosphere they start to decay. Every ozone molecule contains three atoms of oxygen. When it encounters a negatively charged ion of elements such as chlorine or fluorine, an ozone molecule breaks down into a molecule of oxygen (made up of two atoms) and a positively charged ion of oxygen (ions can be either negatively or positively charged). This oxygen ion joins the chlorine or fluorine ion to form a new compound, and the ozone molecule is no more. With each ozone molecule that disappears, the ozone layer is depleted.

Phasing out CFCs

The harmful effects of CFCs on the ozone layer were first scientifically established in the 1970s, and many countries, led by Sweden, started to phase out their use and replace

them with other gases. Then, in 1985, scientists with the British Antarctic Survey reported an alarming depletion of the ozone layer over Antarctica between September and November – the so-called Antarctic ozone hole. In the years since then, losses of nearly 90 per cent have been recorded at certain levels in the ozone layer above Antarctica during these months.

Press coverage of the Antarctic ozone hole helped to galvanise public opinion and governments, and in 1987 a UN-sponsored international treaty to phase out CFCs was agreed and signed in Montreal, Canada. Although a few countries still use CFCs in some of the products they manufacture, the majority have committed themselves to the Montreal Protocol – widely regarded as one of the most successful treaties of its kind. The ozone layer will not recover immediately, but in time it will start to heal. Providing countries continue to adhere to the Montreal Protocol as they are doing now, the ozone layer should have recovered by around 2050.

SCIENCE SAVES LIVES

Three British scientists, Joseph Farman, Brian Gardiner and Jonathan Shanklin, first reported the Antarctic ozone hole. It is an example of how research into our planet's workings has more than academic importance. Because they understood the function of the ozone layer and were paid to study it, the world was made aware when holes began to appear. Research continues, as here at the US Amundsen-Scott South Pole Station, where scientists are launching a balloon carrying instruments to measure the layer. In the case of the ozone hole, it is certain that science saved lives.

THE WORLD WARMS UP

TWENTY YEARS AGO, GLOBAL WARMING WAS A RELATIVELY NEW IDEA AMONG SCIENTISTS. Some lay people had begun to accept it as a possibility; politicians, generally speaking, dismissed it out of hand. Today, global warming has become a reality that we all have to face. The term global warming is often used interchangeably – and incorrectly – with another: climate change. Although the two phenomena are linked, they are not the same thing. Global warming refers to a rise in the average temperature of the Earth's atmosphere. Climate change, on the other hand, is simply that – a change in climate (the prevailing weather in a certain area). Because a great many factors influence climate, global warming may give rise to climate change in an area, or it may not. Just because the world as a whole warms up does not mean that the weather in a particular part of the globe will, too.

Greenhouse Earth

The cause of global warming is now well known: human activity, particularly the burning of fossil fuels, has led to an increase of greenhouse gases in the atmosphere. Acting like the glass in a greenhouse, which lets sunlight in but not heat out, a

HONG KONG GRIDLOCK Cars are one of the biggest contributors to global warming. As the number of people on the planet increases, so does the number of cars. Car ownership is rising particularly fast in rapidly developing countries, such as China.

东四十条桥
DONGSISHITIAO Bridge

雍和宫桥
YONGHEGONG QIAO
3km

小街桥
XIAOJIE QIAO
2.5km

东直门桥
DONGZHIMEN QIAO
800m

greenhouse gas prevents heat from the Sun from bouncing back into space after it is reflected off the Earth's surface.

A number of greenhouse gases exist – among them carbon dioxide, methane, nitrous oxide and water vapour – and all occur naturally in the atmosphere. In recent centuries, however, the concentrations of some have increased. Methane levels, for instance, are now significantly higher than they once were. Probable reasons include a rise in rice production using paddy fields, where flooding gives rise to methane through fermentation. At the same time, increasing numbers of livestock give off methane as a digestive by-product, while organic material decomposing in rubbish tips and landfill sites also releases emissions.

Although all the greenhouse gases play their part in global warming, carbon dioxide is by far the biggest contributor to the problem, because its concentration in the atmosphere has risen the most. Carbon dioxide is produced whenever any organic matter is burned. Before people harnessed fire, this happened only as a result of lightning strikes or volcanic activity. The level of carbon dioxide in the atmosphere was stable. Nowadays, we burn vast quantities of organic matter every day. Wood goes up in smoke in our fires and wherever slash-and-burn farmers clear land. Coal and oil, both fossilised organic materials, are burned in even greater quantities, along with another fossil fuel – natural gas.

Wasteful lifestyles

The biggest contributors to the increase in carbon dioxide levels are the inhabitants of industrialised nations. The modern Western lifestyle burns enormous volumes of energy in powering cars, generating electricity and heating homes. The manufacture and distribution of most products is also a significant factor. Coal, gas and oil fuel modern consumer societies.

The average European or North American uses far more fossil fuel than most people elsewhere, even without owning a car. Other nations, however, are catching up. In 2007, China became the world's biggest producer of greenhouse gases, knocking the United States off the ignominious top spot it had occupied for decades. The position went to China as a nation. Calculated per head of population, China's fossil fuel consumption is still far less than in the West. But China is home to nearly a fifth of the world's population and the amount they use is rising as the country's economy grows.

Legend:
- Built-up land
- Nuclear energy
- Carbon dioxide from fossil fuels
- Fishing ground
- Forest
- Grazing land
- Cropland

y-axis: Hectares per person, 2003

Countries (left to right): UAE, USA, FINLAND, CANADA, AUSTRALIA, FRANCE, UK, IRELAND, GERMANY, RUSSIA, JAPAN, MEXICO, BRAZIL, CHINA, NIGERIA, INDONESIA, INDIA, SOMALIA, AFGHANISTAN

ECOLOGICAL FOOTPRINT People's ecological 'footprints' can be measured by the amount of biologically productive land and sea it takes to supply their needs and absorb their waste. The graph below shows the average footprint per person for a number of countries in 2003 – not surprisingly, individuals from developed countries have a far larger footprint than people from poorer nations. The global average is around 1.8 hectares per person. Citizens of the United Arab Emirates (UAE) use more than six times than that – almost 12 hectares. At the other end of the scale, people from Afghanistan each use less than a quarter of a hectare.

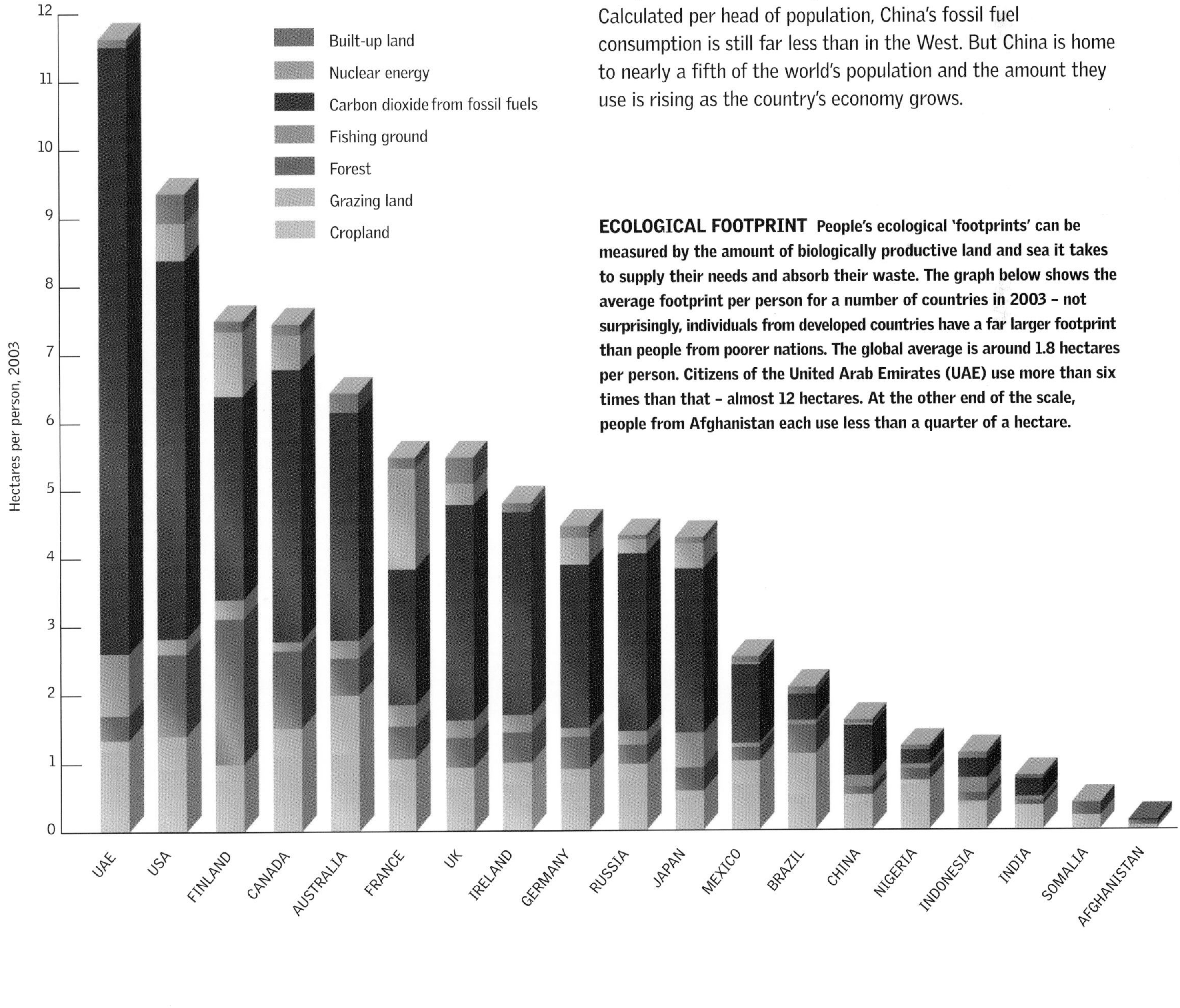

SNOW REFLECTS LIGHT AND HEAT

WHERE THE SNOW MELTS, THE DARKER ICE ABSORBS MORE HEAT AND MELTS MORE QUICKLY

RETREATING ICE The Middle Rongbu Glacier once filled this valley in the high Himalayas. In common with glaciers around the world, it has shrunk as global temperatures have risen.

THINNER ICE HAS A WEAKER GRIP ON THE BEDROCK, WHICH CANNOT HOLD BACK THE GLACIER

MELTWATER FRACTURES THE ICE, PLUNGES INTO THE RESULTING CREVASSES AND LUBRICATES THE BOTTOM OF THE GLACIER

WARM OCEAN CURRENTS EAT AWAY AT THE ICE, CAUSING THINNER PORTIONS TO BREAK UP

ATTACK ON DIFFERENT FRONTS

The disappearance of glaciers is a complex process, with several factors affecting the way that they melt. These include rising snow lines on mountainsides, which leave areas of ice exposed. Being darker in colour than snow, the ice absorbs more heat and melts more quickly. At the same time, glaciers that reach the ocean are threatened by both rising sea temperatures and warmer air above them.

Contributing to the production of greenhouse gases and so to global warming is hard to avoid in the modern world. Emissions from power stations make up more than 20 per cent of the greenhouse gases produced every year; most countries have coal-fired power stations and many rely on them for the bulk of their electricity supply. The burning of transport fuel, much of it consumed by aircraft and ships moving goods, accounts for 14 per cent. Industrial processes produce almost 17 per cent and waste disposal and treatment just over 3 per cent. More than 11 per cent of global greenhouse gas emissions are generated by the retrieval, processing and distribution of fossil fuels themselves – that's before they are even burned.

Global warming is already changing the Earth. At present, the effects are still relatively minor, but if emissions continue at current rates, that could change. The biggest threat to people is rising sea levels. As the world warms up, glaciers retreat and the icecaps melt. Water that was once frozen makes its way into the oceans, threatening low-lying islands and coasts and affecting the circulation of ocean currents.

Disappearing islands

In the past 100 years, sea levels have risen by around 15 cm and the rate at which they are climbing is accelerating. The inhabitants of the low-lying Pacific island nation of Nauru are getting used to the sea flooding their homes every time there is a storm. In the late 1990s, two uninhabited atolls belonging to the Pacific island nation of Kiribati vanished altogether beneath the waves. Then, in December 2006, Lohachara Island, in the delta of India's Ganges River, was reported as the first formerly inhabited island to vanish completely as a result of recent sea level rise. The island had once been home to hundreds of families, but they left in the 1980s once the slow inundation was clearly under way.

Lohachara Island could be just a foretaste of what is to come. Recent studies have focused on the Greenland icecap, which if it melted entirely would cause an estimated sea level rise of 7 m – enough to flood many low-lying cities, including Los Angeles, London and Hong Kong. According to scientists, a global temperature rise of 3°C is all that it would take for this to happen. In the last century the average global temperature rose by 0.6°C. Even if that rate of temperature rise stayed the same – rather than increased, as is expected – Greenland could be ice-free within 500 years. Five centuries might seem like a long time, but the melt, and the sea level rise, would be steady and sure. And Greenland would not be alone – the rest of the Earth's icecaps would be melting, too.

We tend to focus on the effect that global warming will have on us, yet it has already begun to alter the rest of the natural world. In mountain ranges, the altitude at which trees grow is slowly getting higher, and other plants and animals are beginning to live farther up the slopes. The geographical ranges of plants and animals are moving nearer to the Poles, at a rate of just over 6 km per decade. A further change is the advance of spring. By the end of the 20th century, spring was arriving on average 2.3 days earlier every decade in temperate parts of the world.

WORSENING PROBLEM Low-lying islands such as Tuvalu in the Pacific Ocean are the first to suffer from rising sea levels. When high tides combine with storms, large areas may be flooded. Once rare, such sea floods are becoming ever more common.

AN UNCERTAIN FUTURE

BLUE SKY THINKING Eco-friendly housing can help to combat global warming and be attractive, too, as shown in the Netherlands by this development of homes powered with solar energy.

IN THE 20TH CENTURY, THE WORLD CHANGED MORE THAN IT HAD DONE OVER THE COURSE OF MILLIONS OF YEARS BEFORE THAT. In the 21st century, there is the prospect that it will change even more. The current rate of shrinkage of the Arctic icecap, for example, is 8 per cent a decade, and with global temperatures set to rise even faster than they are today, that rate is likely to increase. Since the Arctic icecap floats on top of the Arctic Ocean, its disappearance would not greatly affect sea levels, but the Arctic environment would alter entirely. Creatures such as the polar bear, which rely on sea ice to survive, would almost certainly face extinction.

The sea rises

The Arctic icecap aside, glaciers and snow lines are retreating all over the globe. Potentially, along with dwindling land-based icecaps, such as Greenland's, this phenomenon has far more serious consequences for us. The meltwater from these sources could cause sea levels to rise by several metres this century alone. Even a much smaller increase would change coastlines, with the rate of erosion increasing as waves wash up over beaches and crash against cliffs more frequently. Most city-dwellers should be protected by new flood defences, at least in the developed world, but for people outside cities already facing the onslaught of the sea, things are likely to get worse.

Climate change as a result of global warming will almost certainly kick in. In some areas of the world, rainfall will decrease, reducing water supplies and threatening harvests; in others, heavy rain will become more frequent, causing low-lying areas to flood. Some of the greatest changes could occur in western Europe, which at present enjoys relatively mild winters as a result of the warm waters brought to its shores by the Gulf Stream. Global warming could cause the path of the Gulf Stream to shift. Cold water entering the North Atlantic from the melting Arctic icecap could push it southwards, or possibly even halt its northern end entirely, bringing the warming current to a stop in mid-ocean. Either way, Britain and its Continental neighbours would face Moscow-style winters.

Global warming is likely to change all of our lives, and certainly the lives of the next generation. Other trends that look set to continue include population growth and deforestation. Cities will swell, and wilderness areas continue to shrink. Our growing numbers mean that we will have more and more impact on the Earth's natural systems, although it is doubtful that we will have any more control over them. Even so, humankind is nothing if not adaptable and we will almost certainly find solutions to some of the problems posed to us by a changing world. The threat to other species is likely to increase, and as habitats shrink, extinctions will follow. Life as a whole, however, will survive and evolution will continue. The world may change, but it has been through far greater changes before.

Global warming could cause the path of the Gulf Stream to shift. Cold water entering the North Atlantic from the melting Arctic icecap could push it southwards or possibly even bring it to a stop mid-ocean. Either way, Britain and its Continental neighbours would face Moscow-style winters.

THE FOLKS WHO LIVE IN THE HILL

As pressure increases to reduce our dependence on fossil fuels and our impact on the Earth, more sustainable building methods and design techniques are emerging. The 'earth sheltering' technique started in the USA in 1973 and entails building into, rather than onto, the landscape. Yorkshire architect Arthur Quarmby introduced it to Britain in 1975, when he built a home, 'Underhill' (below), near Holmfirth on the fringes of the Peak District National Park.

There is nothing new about humans living underground – they have done so since prehistory and still do in some parts of the world. But high-specification, modern underground houses represent a new trend in harnessing the environmental advantages of subterranean living. These include energy efficiency. With the house surrounded on three sides by soil, there is little or no need for space heating. Warmth from the soil, which retains heat longer than the air, lodges in the building's walls and is transferred to the interior, along the lines of a storage heater. Temperatures in the house remain stable, further cutting heating requirements.

Plentiful and efficient glazing allows heat and light in, while preventing most of the heat from escaping; it can also be linked to a system for heating water. At the same time, building into the ground makes the house less obtrusive, saves land surface space and allows plant life to resettle. Earth sheltering homes are also spared the ravages of extreme weather.

INDEX

PICTURE CREDITS

Abbreviations: T = top; B = bottom; L = left; R = right
Front cover: Science Photo Library/NASA/ESA/ N. Smith University of California, Berkeley/Hubble Heritage Team (STSCL/AURA)
Back cover: naturepl.com/Anup Shah

1 DRK Photo/Doug Perrine. **2-7** Science Photo Library/Robert Gendler. **3** N.A.Sharp/NOAO/ AURA/NSF, T; NASA/Jet Propulsion Laboratory, MR. **4** Science Photo Library/Michael Abbey. **5** FLPA/Chris Mattison, B; Corbis/Louie Psihoyos, MR. **6** Shutterstock/Marina Cano Trueba, T; Science Photo Library/James A.Hancock B. **8-9** Corbis/Danny Lehman. **10-11** NASA/European Space Agency/J. Hester, 1; naturepl/Aflo, 2; naturepl.com/Pete Oxford, 3; David Doubilet/ www.daviddoubilet.com, 4; Still Pictures/Fritz Polking, 5; Science Photo Library/Bernhard Edmaier, 6; DRK Photo/T.A. Wiewandt, 7. **12-13** Olivier Grunewald, background; left to right: Photoshot/NHPA/Stephen Dalton, NASA/JPL-Caltech/SSC/Susan Stolovy, Auscape/Jurgen Freund, naturepl.com/Anup Shah, Auscape/John Cancalosi, photolibrary.com/Mark Jones. **14-15** NASA/ESA/J. Hester. **16** NASA/WMAP Science Team. **17** Science Photo Library/NASA/ ESA/HDF Team, R. Williams. **18** NASA/ESA and the Hubble Heritage Team STScI/AURA. **19** NASA/JPL-Caltech/SSC/Susan Stolovy. **20-21** NASA/ESA and Jesus Maiz Apellaniz (Instituto de Astrofisica de Andalucia, Spain). **22** NASA/JPL/Malin Space Science System, B. **23** NASA/ESA/SOHO. **24** Science Photo Library/US Geological Survey, L; NASA/JPL, ML; NASA/Goddard Space Flight Centre/Reto Stockli, MR; NASA, R. **24-25** NASA/Hubble Heritage Team. **25** NASA/Hubble Heritage Team, L; ML; MR; Science Photo Library/Friedrich Saurer, R. **27** NASA, R. **28-29** photolibrary.com/Olivier Grunewald. **29** Science Photo Library/Jerry Lodriguss. **30-31** Olivier Grunewald. **32-33** Robert Harding/Global Pictures. **33** ESA/DLR/FU Berlin/G. Neukum. **34-35** Olivier Grunewald. **36** Corbis/ Zefa/Werner H. Mueller. **37** Photoshot/NHPA/ Stephen Dalton, T; National Image Collection/Joel Sartore, B. **38** NASA/Science Photo Library. **38-39** naturepl.com/Aflo. **39** DSV Alvin Dive 4051, 2004, East Pacific Rise/NSF/ courtesy of Mitchell Schulte, T. **40** Institute of Geological and Nuclear Sciences/Bruce Mountain. **41** Corbis/Jonathan Blair, T; Photoshot/NHPA/ Imagequest 3D, M; Science Photo Library/Alfred Pasieka, B. **42** Still Pictures/Roland Birke. **43** naturepl/Solvin Zanki. **44** FLPA/Reinard Dirscherl. **45** naturepl.com/Jeff Rotman, T; FLPA/Minden Pictures/Flip Nicklin. B. **46** Auscape/Jurgen Freund. **47** Photoshot/NHPA/ Imagequest 3-D, T; Science Photo Library/Steve Gschmeissner, B. **48** Photoshot/NHPA/Stephen Dalton. **49** Premaphoto/Ken Preston-Mafham. **50-51** National Geographic Image Collection/Tim Laman. **52** Auscape/Tom Till. **53** Still Pictures/Ed Reschke. **54** Auscape/Pavel German. **55** naturepl.com/John Waters. **56** Still Pictures/ Kevin Schafer. **57** FLPA/Minden Pictures/Frans Lanting. **58** naturepl.com/Dave Watts. **59** Corbis/Robert Pickett, T; DRK Photo/Mike & Lisa Husar, B. **60** FLPA/Foto Natura/Flip de Nooyer, T; DRK Photo/Wayne Lynch, B. **61** Corbis/ Louie Psihoyos. **62-63** DRK Photo/Martin Harvey. **63** FLPA/Winfried Wisniewski. T. **64-65** FLPA/ Jurgen & Christine Sohns. **65** photolibrary.com/ Gerard Soury. **66** ardea.com/Adrian Warren, L; Wessex Archaeology, R. **67** Science Photo Library/ John Reader. **68** Corbis/DK Ltd/Colin Keates, Palaeozoic Arthropod; Science Photo Library/ Sinclair Stammers, First Fossils; Hans Hofmann/ McGill University, Algae; Digitalvision, Earth Strip. **69** Corbis/James L. Amos, First Birds; Corbis/ Louie Psihoyos, Triasic Arrival; Topfoto/ ImageWorks, Sabre Teeth; Digitalvision, FernStrip. **70-71** Hedgehog House/Pat Barrett. **72** Lonely Planet Images/Lee Foster. **73** Still Pictures/ Rosemary Calvert. **74** ardea.com/Auscape/Jean-Paul Ferrero. **75** Science Photo Library/NASA, T;

Olivier Grunewald, BR. **76-77** FLPA/Gary K. Smith. **78-79** ardea.com/Bill Coster. **79** Getty Images/Gay Bumgarner. **80-81** naturepl.com/Pete Oxford. **81** naturepl.com/Dave Watts, R. **82-83** DRK Photo/Stephen G. Maka. **84-85** National Geographic Image Collection/Norbert Rosing. **86-87** National Geographic Image Collection/Norbert Rosing. **87** Science Photo Library/Dr Kari Lounatmaa, R. **88-89** Photoshot/ NHPA/Martin Harvey. **89** Photoshot/NHPA/ Manfred Danegger, T; DRK Photo/Fred Bruemmer, B. **90** National Geographic Image Collection/Annie Griffiths Belt. **91** National Geographic Image Collection/Jim & Jamie Dutcher. **92** naturepl.com/ Phil Savoie. **92-93** ardea.com/Francois Gohier. **94** National Geographic Image Collection/Roy Toft. **95** Auscape/Tui de Roy. **96** David Doubilet/ www.daviddoubilet.com. **97** naturepl.com/Solvin Zanki. **98** National Geographic Image Collection/ Des & Jen Bartlett. **99** National Geographic Image Collection/Jim Richardson, T; David Doubilet/ www.daviddoubilet.com, B. **100-101** B & C Alexander/Arcticphoto.com. **101** David Doubilet/ www.daviddoubilet.com. **102** FLPA/Minden Pictures/Mitsuaki Iwago. **103** naturepl.com/Anup Shah. **104-105** naturepl.com/Mark Carwardine. **106-107** Auscape/John Cancalosi. **108-109** Still Pictures/Fritz Polking. **109** DRK Photo/John Cancalosi. **110-111** ardea.com/Francois Gohier. **111** ardea.com/Francois Gohier. **112** Science Photo Library/George Steinmetz. **113** Richard Martin. **114** Corbis/Jonathan Blair, T; R. **114-115** Corbis/ Zefa/Jorma Jaemsen (background). **115** Science Photo Library/Martin Land, TL; Corbis/Jonathan Blair, TR; DRK Photo/John Cancalosi, ML; DRK Photo/T.A. Wiewandt, BL; Corbis/DK/Colin Keates, BR. **116-117** Science Photo Library/Bernhard Edmaier. **118** photolibrary.com/Ken Wagner, T; Corbis/James L. Amos, B. **119** naturepl.com/John Cancalosi, T; Corbis/Jonathan Blair, L; Corbis/Louie Psihoyos, BR. **120** photolibrary.com/Liysa. **121** PA Photos/AP/David Vais. **122** South American Pictures/Kimball Morrison. **123** Photoshot/NHPA/ Stephen Dalton. **124-125** FLPA/Minden Pictures/ Richard du Toit. **125** Corbis/Gary Braasch. **126-127** photolibrary.com/Mark Jones. **128-129** Getty Images/Lanz von Horsten. **130-131** Corbis/Jason Hawkes. **132** Reuters/Kyoshi Ota. **132-133** National Geographic Image Collection/Joy Tessman. **134** National Geographic Image Collection/Joel Sartore. **135** Corbis/AJ/ IRRI, ML; Auscape/Hedgehog House, BR. **136-137** DRK Photo/T. A. Wiewandt. **138-139** FLPA/Minden Pictures/JH Editorial/Cyril Ruoso. **140** FLPA/Paul Hobson. **140-141** Corbis/ Yann Arthus-Bertrand. **142** Natural England/Peter Wakely, ML; Alamy/Dominic Burke, B. **143** NASA/ Goddard Space Flight Center/Scientific Visualization Studio. **144** FLPA/Minden Pictures/ Frans Lanting. **145** FSC-UK, TR; FLPA/Minden Pictures/Frans Lanting, B. **146** Corbis/Paul A. Souders. **147** Camera Press/Gamma/Thierry Falise. **148** Science Photo Library/NASA. **149** PA Photos/ AP/NASA, T; Hutchison/Eye Ubiquitous/Laurence Fordyce, B. **150** Rex Features/Arcaid. **152** © Greenpeace/John Novis, T. **153** Gary Braasch. **154-155** Still Pictures/Martin Bond.

Artworks
3-6 J.B. Illustrations
20, 26-27, 68-69, 152 Glyn Walton LINEDESIGN
22 Bradbury & Williams
72 Mountain High Maps
151 Bradbury & Williams, based on *Living Planet Report 2006*, published in October 2006 by World Wide Fund For Nature

NATURE'S MIGHTY POWERS: FORCES OF CHANGE was published by The Reader's Digest Association Ltd, London. It was created and produced for Reader's Digest by Toucan Books Ltd, London.

The Reader's Digest Association Ltd,
11 Westferry Circus,
Canary Wharf,
London E14 4HE
www.readersdigest.co.uk

First edition copyright © 2008

Written by
Daniel Gilpin

FOR TOUCAN BOOKS
Editors Jane Chapman, Helen Douglas-Cooper, Leon Gray, Andrew Kerr-Jarrett, Chris Marshall
Designers Bradbury & Williams
Picture researchers Wendy Brown, Sharon Southren, Mia Stewart-Wilson, Christine Vincent, Caroline Wood
Proofreader Marion Dent
Indexer Michael Dent

FOR READER'S DIGEST
Project editor Christine Noble
Art editor Julie Bennett
Pre-press account manager Penny Grose
Product production manager Claudette Bramble
Production controller Katherine Bunn

READER'S DIGEST, GENERAL BOOKS
Editorial director Julian Browne
Art director Anne-Marie Bulat

Colour origination Colour Systems Ltd, London
Printed and bound in China

We are committed to both the quality of our products and the service we provide to our customers. We value your comments, so please feel free to contact us on 08705 113366 or via our website at **www.readersdigest.co.uk**

If you have any comments or suggestions about the content of our books, you can email us at **gbeditorial@readersdigest.co.uk**

CONCEPT CODE: UK0138/G/S
BOOK CODE: 636-006 UP0000-1
ISBN: 978-0-276-44294-0
ORACLE CODE: 356500008H.00.24